SEO in the Gemini Era

The story of how AI Changed Google Search

by Dr. Marie Haynes.

June 2024

This book goes along with these resources:

If you purchased a bundle, you should have received an email with instructions for accessing all of the files. Otherwise, you can purchase these resources individually here:

- Workbook: Put Yourself in the Shoes of a Searcher
- Workbook: Traffic Drop Diagnosis & Advice (Free)
- Course: SEO in the Gemini Era. (Much more detail on the machine learning systems behind search, more exercises and a detailed plan for producing topical authority.)
- See all products and bundles

Questions about this book? Find me in the Search Bar.

Brainstorm with Marie

Table of Contents

SEO in the Gemini Era
    The story of how AI Changed Google Search

Table of Contents

A little history: How SEO worked before AI changed the game
    For site owners trying to recover following a Google update
    About Marie

Part 1: AI has changed how Search works

A mindset shift is needed for SEOs
    People first content is:

Navboost: Google's use of user engagement signals
    My understanding of how ranking works in 2024:
    How does this information change how we create content on our websites?
    You made it this far!

Links. How Google values them has changed.
    Are links still used in Google's ranking systems?
    My thoughts on links
    New information from Google's API docs "leak"
    Here are my current thoughts on links
        The mismatch between black hat SEOs who have success building links and white hats who do not
    Should you build links?
    Is this a good link?

Topical Authority, the Knowledge graph, and its topic layer
    Why I believe we need to pay attention to topical authority

    The knowledge graph
    The next generation of search
        Gemini
Structured data
    Is schema a ranking factor?
        The topic layer of the knowledge graph (again)
    The experiences of the SEO community
    What about AI? Where does structured data fit in?
Intent (and oh boy let's talk vector embeddings, fine-tuning and more)
    Vector embeddings
    Transformers
    BERT
    Fine-tuning
    RankEmbed BERT
    What happens when keywords are replaced by attributes?
    Simplifying all of this
        How do you know what the intents and microintents of your audience are?
Part 2: People-First Content
Effort
Audience. The importance of being known for your topics
        A side note about spam
        You may need to build an audience
    How do you become known?
Freshness
Hidden Gems
Experience
    What is real world experience?
        Sites with customers in the offline world

    Known topic experts

    You have used a product or service

Looking ahead to the future - SGE, Gemini...and AGI?

    Google's Search Generative Experience / AI Overviews.

    Google Gemini (formerly Bard)

  Business integration

  AGI / ASI

A new age for content...and everything really!

I'm going to tell you the story of Google's remarkable journey from lines of code written by students, into a sophisticated AI system that is becoming more and more the source of information on current events, healthcare advice, and learning information to shape our knowledge and beliefs.

Google has spent the last 25 years learning how to organize the world's information and make it universally accessible and useful[1].

---

[1] About Google. https://www.google.com/search/howsearchworks/our-approach.2024.

> Our mission is to organize the world's information and make it universally accessible and useful.

It has been an honour being a part of the development of a helpful and reliable web that has become the foundation of a powerful AI system that truly is moving closer and closer to becoming what many call AGI - Artificial General Intelligence. Google has been building towards AGI, and this is why the effort to organize the world's information holds immense responsibility.

This book is written primarily for my friends and colleagues who call ourselves SEOs, an incredibly intelligent group of people who are good at understanding how search engines work and what it is that they are built to reward. However, anyone with an interest in how search engines work should find it interesting! Boy has AI changed Google - right under our noses, and we are about to see a lot more changes that will impact the lives of all who are reading this book.

We are in a wild time of change. Most of this book focuses on understanding how search works and just what a big role AI plays, so that we can improve our chances of creating websites and content that will get found online. The last bit of the book goes well beyond working to shift websites around in ranking positions to higher ranking positions, to discuss what it means for the world when Google's AI is in our earbuds, and potentially even one day, controlled by our thoughts. This might seem like a scary idea, especially if you currently are seeing your search results filled with spam and commercially incentivized content.

It is so important for Google to learn how to truly recommend content that searchers find helpful and reliable.

This is why Google's machine learning systems - AI systems - continue to do what they are built to do...steadily learn and improve.

This whole idea of organizing the world's information in the form of what we now know as Google, came to be because of an idea that came to Stanford student Larry Page in a dream. He woke up in the middle of the night, in the middle of a dream in which he thought, "What if we could download the whole web, and just keep the links?[2]" Shortly after, Google was born.

Links. Oh SEOs love links don't we? We'll talk about links and I'll share how I think they are used by Google's systems today.

It has bothered me for years that there is such a mismatch between the beliefs of the SEOs I know who build links, and those who do their work without link building. One crowd has loads of evidence to show that building links moves the needle for them. Another, which includes the majority of the

---

[2] Larry Page at University of Michigan. https://whatrocks.github.io/commencement-db/2009-larry-page-university-of-michigan/. 2009.

SEOs and site owners that I have worked with and known over the years, have found that while there once was a day where link building was a powerful SEO tool, it has far fewer returns today, unless perhaps you can get truly good, authoritative mentions. I'm talking about the kind of link that you screenshot and share with your parents because you can't believe you got mentioned there.

I believe I can explain this mismatch today. I believe both camps are correct. Links are very important if you are creating content primarily for search engines. However, if you are creating content for a hungry audience, then I believe links play a completely different role. I'll share much more in the links section of this book.

I'll also share detailed thoughts on topical authority. It is incredibly important. If you really are creating content that is born out of the needs of your audience, you probably have already created a body of topical authority.

We will also talk about schema as this has been something that has been a difficult area for me to understand over the years. Google tells us it's not important to ranking and yet they tell us it's important to use. It turns out that schema plays a big role in helping machines understand content. We absolutely should be paying attention to schema.

My favourite part of this book is the chapter on intent. It gets pretty technical. I've worked for months with both ChatGPT and Bard/Gemini and a whole lot of research papers to not only understand how machine learning systems understand intent, but also to be able to explain it as simply as possible.

This section also takes you on a journey of learning incredibly exciting things like vector embeddings, reinforcement learning and fine-tuning. Learning about how LLM based systems like ChatGPT and Gemini improve themselves by learning from user conversations has been fascinating. If you have tried these tools and found them lacking, know that they are steadily improving and will continue to do so. What we can and will do with AI chatbots is terribly exciting!

Part two of this book is specifically written to content creators. We will delve through the importance of building an audience, producing fresh content, demonstrating your experience in unique and insightful ways and most of all, creating content that clearly has had a lot of *effort* put into it.

And then, after you've read my ramblings for a couple of hundred pages, I'm going to tell you why much of this is unlikely to matter a decade or so from now. A whole book could be written on Google's drive to create what is known as AGI - Artificial General Intelligence. AGI is AI that can accomplish any cognitive tasks a human can.

It is almost impossible to wrap our heads around how AGI will change our world. Especially when we've seen enough movies where AI is a malevolent force, a Terminator coming to wreak havoc and potentially destroy the world.

Humans do not like change. We especially do not like change that comes with potential risk.

By now you are likely well aware of many of the potential risks that go along with the development of AI. Images and videos that are getting more and more indiscernible from reality can be generated with a simple text prompt. AI enables bad actors to scam people via phone calls and to find all sorts of new ways to get spam in front of you, whether it's in your inbox, your search results or really, anywhere.

These risks and many others are incredibly real. In March of 2023, many AI leaders signed a petition asking the world to [pause training of AI systems for a period of time](#)[3]. The petition urged,

"Advanced AI could represent a profound change in the history of life on Earth, and should be planned for and managed with commensurate care and resources. Unfortunately, this level of planning and management is not happening, even though recent months have seen AI labs locked in an out-of-control race to develop and deploy ever more powerful digital minds that no one – not even their creators – can understand, predict, or reliably control."

We are moving so quickly when it comes to AI innovations, and it's unlikely that this pace will slow down. In fact, the opposite will happen!

---

[3] Pause Giant AI Experiments: An Open Letter. https://futureoflife.org/open-letter/pause-giant-ai-experiments/ March 2023.

There is far more potential for good than for bad with AI. Google's AI team, DeepMind, is on a trajectory that might one day give us an unimaginable future where disease is solved, climate change is solved, and the cost of producing energy is reduced to almost nothing.

It's almost too much to comprehend. Google started with a dream a student programmer had about links on the web. For twenty five years, they have worked to slowly make good on their mission - to organize the world's information and make it universally accessible to all. If you do work as an SEO, you have been a part of this mission. You have worked to help your clients' business and content be included in the body of information that exists in the world and is worthy of recommending to others.

AI has already changed how Google's search results work. I predict we are in the midst of much more rapid and obvious change as Google continues to work towards AGI.

One thing is certain for now. What Google wants and needs is a fresh source of content that people are hungry for. AI will continue to develop. And some websites that exist today will no longer be viable. But for many others, the Gemini era is likely to bring forth exciting changes where Google's systems actively reward truly helpful and reliable content.

Just before publishing this book, something very cool happened to me. I was invited to attend Google's I/O Developer conference, in person, in California. At lunch, a man sat down next to me. I thought, "He looks familiar." I nearly fell off of my chair when I realized the man was Jeff Dean, the co-founder of Google Brain, and now the Chief Scientist leading AI at Google DeepMind. I'll share more at the end of this book about how my conversations with Jeff Dean changed my life, and I hope, yours as well!

Thank you for taking the time to read this book. Your time is precious and I am quite rambly! I do believe you will find it more than worth it to continue. Our world is changing, and those who understand how AI works will be the ones people look to.

Whether you believe it or not, that's you.

A little history: How SEO worked before AI changed the game

Do you remember the first money you made online as a result of SEO?

For me, it happened in 2009.

I was a veterinarian. I thoroughly loved my job.

I loved a challenging diagnostic puzzle. A case I remember well was when I saw a lovely, yet aging Golden Retriever, who was struggling with mobility. This is not uncommon. Several vets had diagnosed the dog with arthritis and prescribed medication. When I saw her, something didn't seem to fit with the pattern of her symptoms. Sure, her hips were weak, but she walked with a different gait than most Goldens with hip arthritis.

Bloodwork showed high calcium levels - not good news for a Golden. This often is a sign of lymphoma, one of the most common causes of death for this breed. But again, the patterns were not right. I had seen many Goldens with lymphoma, and this one felt different.

We pressed on. I did loads of research and came up with some ideas. What else could cause high calcium levels? I dug deep into discussion forums amongst vets on the internet and found some interesting cases where similar symptoms were caused by a tumor in the parathyroid gland - a tiny little collection of cells sitting on this dog's neck. Could it be a parathyroid tumor? They're incredibly rare. A few tests and help from some specialists later confirmed our suspicions. It was a parathyroid tumor! Benign, yet causing all sorts of problems with the body's production of calcium. As calcium is needed for muscle strength, this was the source of the dog's weakness.

A few days after the tumor was removed by a surgical specialist, the dog had completely regained all of her strength.

I really loved my job.

As a brand new graduate, I was vaccinating a litter of new puppies. One, another gorgeous Golden retriever pup, had a very loud wooosh - woooosh - wooooooosh sound as I listened to his heart. A very bad heart murmur. The dog's gums were a mixture of pink and blue. He had all of the signs of a patent ductus arteriosus, a birth defect that causes a part of the heart to form improperly, and also, a sure death sentence if not treated surgically.

The treatment for this condition is open heart surgery and requires a visit to a university hospital equipped to do cardiac surgery -- a very expensive venture.

The owner decided upon euthanasia. I offered another solution. Let me try heart surgery! What's the risk?

I traveled back to my university and spent hours in the library studying how to do this surgery, what materials to use, how to approach the problem and more.

Let me pause here. Do you remember the library? I have so many fond memories of learning in a library.

That surgery was one of the most exciting things I have ever done. I opened the side of the dog's chest and before me was this huge throbbing blood vessel. I could see and feel the turbulent blood flowing wildly through it. This part of a dog's circulation in its heart is supposed to close down naturally at birth. Instead, I gently took my silk suture and tied it around the vessel to see if I could accomplish what nature did not.

The textbooks I checked out from the library told me one of two things was about to happen as I tightened the suture. First, if the walls of the vessel were thin, or if I was too rough, it would rip through the fragile vessel, and the dog would very quickly bleed to death.

As you can probably guess, that did not happen! Instead, as I slowly closed the vessel, the turbulence calmed. I will never forget the feeling. I asked my assistant to hold up the dog's lip so we could see his gums. And wow, they turned from bluish to perfectly pink.

This dog went on to have a long happy goofy Golden Retriever life.

I loved my job..

My job was so interesting.

And today, instead of saving pet lives, I help websites rank on Google.

What the heck?

Let me get back to that first money that I made online. Why would a happy and successful veterinarian try to make money on the internet?

I graduated from vet school in 1999. We learned from textbooks, but you would often find me in the computer lab on a website called Veterinary Information Network - a place where vets could share about interesting cases and brainstorm together on solutions.

It was the internet that made me good at my craft. Access to information gave me a superpower. While other vets were reaching into their memory banks to help them solve cases, I learned to learn from the experiences of other vets shared on the internet.

The same thing is happening today. AI is creating entirely new ways to access information online. Those who learn how to use it have a huge advantage. My hope is that this book inspires you to learn more about AI. There is so much opportunity ahead of us. We are going to talk a lot about how AI has changed Google's search algorithms. But this is just the start. AI is completely changing how humans interact with technology.

The deluge of veterinary misinformation that was available online was what drove me to create my first website. I was tired of having conversations with my clients who had read bad advice on the internet.

"I've been treating my dog with garlic for fleas because that's what Yahoo! Answers says is best." Meanwhile, garlic is toxic to a dog's red blood cells.

"It's 3 am and my dog has bloody diarrhea and the internet tells me he is about to die if I don't see you right now." Let me tell you, there are many things that can cause bloody diarrhea in a dog, and most of them are not at all serious. If your dog has bloody diarrhea, but is still bounding around like a maniac, you'll do just as well with a short fasting period followed by bland food for a couple of days than with a middle of the night emergency vet visit.

As a fun project to work on in the evenings, I learned some HTML, PHP and CSS from a tutorial on About.com and bit by bit cobbled together a veterinary Q&A website. Then I had an idea. What if I could charge people a small fee to answer their veterinary questions online? Perhaps I could make a living by helping others online? And in doing so I could put good, trustworthy information on the web.

After a long bout of reading, testing, going to bed frustrated (oh how many times was I missing a semi-colon in my code), and trying over and over again, I finally got Paypal integration to work on my website. For $5 anyone in the world could ask me a question about their pet.

The next day, I got an email.

NEW $5 QUESTION….

omg. Someone paid real money because of something I created online.

Then I saw the question. It was my husband, David.

"When are you coming to bed?"

☐

I had this great website with a bunch of useful information on it. Sure, it wasn't the prettiest, but damn it was the information on it helpful. It was better than what existed elsewhere, and no one was coming to it.

I went on a learning journey again to understand more about how to get people to find my website in Google search. I learned about this thing called SEO - Search Engine Optimization - making your website look good to search engines. I hung out in forums - the Moz Q&A and also the SEO Chat Forums, which sadly, no longer exist today, and learned as much as I could from people who were sharing how they succeeded with SEO.

It seemed that links were one of the most important things that moved the needle. At that time, it didn't take much. I added the words "online veterinary advice" to the signature that appeared below forum posts where allowed. At the time everyone would seek out forums that allowed for followed links in your signature. I quickly learned that too much self promotion gets you kicked out of forums!

I found places like one called Ezine articles where I could write short veterinary articles and link back to my website with words like, "ask a vet" as the anchor text.

I saw a bit of traction.

One day, I was out in the park with my toddler daughter. My Blackberry Curve (you know the one with the actual keyboard - so much nostalgia) pinged - NEW $5 QUESTION.

This time it was for real! The question was "My dog has a red membrane on the corner of its eye." While I can't legally diagnose online, I could say the same sorts of things that I would say if someone who wasn't my client asked me this question. Like if you asked me a question about your pet at a party. There was a good chance this was a "cherry eye", a prolapse of the third eyelid. Sometimes it needs surgery to be fixed. Sometimes it goes away on its own. It's not an emergency, although, as with all of my answers, I finished with the recommendation that the dog be checked out in person with a veterinarian. I had to be careful to not give any medical advice that required a client patient relationship. The idea was to answer questions like I would if a friend at a party asked me a question about their pet.

I was getting the odd question and the traffic I was getting from Google was slowly improving, but not as much as I'd like.

This is when I made a decision that skyrocketed my traffic.

I offered to answer questions for free. I raised the price for paid questions to $20 if you wanted a guaranteed response that day. Free questions piled in. Every day I would spend a couple of hours choosing the questions that would be most likely to help many people and answering them. Thus producing excellent helpful content.

Eventually, a few years later, I had a stockpile of over 3000 veterinary questions that I had answered online. The content was helpful, because rather than being inspired by keyword research, it was borne out of actual questions that my audience had. The more content I produced, the more traffic I got and, the better my rankings got.

My site was written about in Woman's World magazine and had a lot of word of mouth recommendations. I was quoted in several news articles, without me hiring a PR firm or doing journalist outreach. I kept learning to optimize and things kept improving. I had Google Adsense on the site and between that and the paid questions, it was making me a very nice side income - almost, but not quite, enough to live on if I wanted to take time off from veterinary practice.

Today if you look at the site[4], it's a little embarrassing. It still has footer links from an internal linking experiment I started and never finished. There are far too many ads. Sometimes the HTML breaks (there are more </divs> than there should be so one day I just tested adding random ones in places until it worked.) And you can probably find links encouraging you to check out our entry to the Wix SEO competition that helped my team and I win $25,000 by ranking a Wix site for the term "wix seo"[5][6] a few years ago.

Check out Semrush's daily traffic estimates for my veterinary site. This is a fascinating graph. You can see how my efforts at learning how to do well on Google were incredibly rewarding, until 2017.

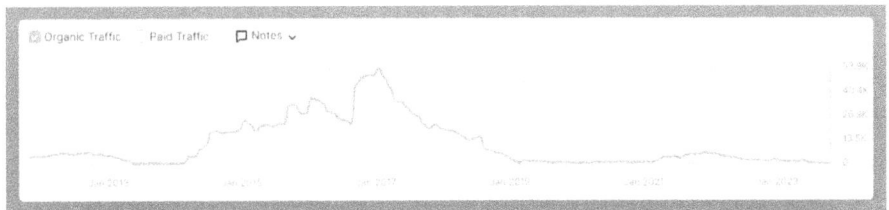

2017 was a big year for Google. 2017 was when I stopped working on my veterinary site and started a company that worked hard to understand Google's search systems.

A lot of things started to change around this time.

---

[4] Ask A Vet Question. Marie Haynes. http://www.askavetquestion.com/

[5] Ding ding ding! We have a winner. Wix Twitter account. Dec 19, 2019. https://x.com/Marie_Haynes/status/1750914226699243904?s=20

[6] Closing thoughts on the Wix SEO competition, and how we made our final push. Alec Brownscombe. Dec 30, 2019. https://www.mariehaynes.com/closing-thoughts-on-the-wix-seo-competition/

2017 was when Google published the research that would change the field of artificial intelligence - a paper called "Attention is all you need.[7]" Google developed technology called the Transformer, a neural network architecture that suddenly opened up so many possibilities for ingenuity because it allowed us to better understand language. The transformer architecture is the foundation of any of the AI tools you use today, including OpenAI's ChatGPT.

In February of 2024, Google developed another new AI architecture called Gemini 1.5 that uses something called a Mixture of Experts model, which as we will talk about shortly, greatly improves their AI capabilities once again. Remember I told you I chatted with Jeff Dean, head of AI at Google? He co-authored the paper on sparsely gated mixture of experts layers[8]. During our lunch together we talked a lot on how the brain is essentially a sparse MoE.

Google says they have been an AI first company since 2016[9].

This doesn't mean that Google flipped a switch and suddenly had an AI powered search engine. Rather, bit by bit they started to implement changes that made use of machine learning using the transformer architecture. We are going to

---

[7] Attention is All You Need. Google. June 2017.
https://arxiv.org/abs/1706.03762

[8] Outrageously Large Neural Networks: The Sparsely-Gated-Mixture-of-Experts Layer.

[9] Google I/O 2023: Making AI more helpful for everyone. Google. May 2023.
https://blog.google/intl/en-africa/company-news/google-io-2023-making-ai-more-helpful-for-everyone/

talk about these AI systems a lot in this book. The recent DOJ vs Google antitrust trial has given us some testimony from Google's Pandu Nayak that tells us a lot about how many AI systems are used to help Google achieve their goal of providing the searcher with helpful and reliable information.

Hopefully as you read this book, you'll realize that much of what we focus on for SEO is not what Google's systems reward today. Many of the things that made my veterinary website successful worked because I learned to do things in the name of SEO that took advantage of the Google search algorithms that existed before AI changed how Google ranks results.

(Although much of the losses the site saw happened because I stopped working on the site as I started and ran an SEO agency from 2017 to 2022.)

I suspect that many of the things that you are doing in the name of SEO today no longer provide the same returns as they did for you a year or more ago.

My hope is that by the end of this book you will have an advantage over those who have not read it and do not understand just how much AI changed Google's results and where Google is headed. There are plenty of opportunities ahead.

Over the last 16 years of thoroughly studying Google's algorithms and systems, brainstorming with site owners,

and continually testing new theories, here is what I believe what it takes to rank in 2024:

1. Be legitimately recognized as a go-to source for your topic.

2. Create content, or a website that people truly find helpful.

I think soon you can possibly succeed with just the second point. But for now, in order to do well on search, you need to provide signals to show Google that people legitimately are finding your content helpful when they want information on the topics you cover. That's hard to do without an audience.

For site owners trying to recover following a Google update

It is getting more and more difficult to recover for sites impacted by a Google update.

This book initially set out to be a guide for the many who have been impacted by AI driven updates - the helpful content updates, core updates and reviews updates. As I wrote it I realized that in order to understand what happened, whether it is possible to recover, and how to do so, you really need to understand how AI has changed search. And boy there is a lot to know!

As such, I've moved the recovery info to its own [workbook](). This workbook is available to anyone for no charge.

For some sites impacted, if you are willing to put in significant hard work, I believe that Google's "hidden gems" system is set to reward some excellent content. This book will help you know how to create that content and will show you some examples of where this type of helpful content is starting to appear in Google's search results.

We'll talk about the types of things you can do to possibly recover. Although in many cases when we see nice improvements like this, it's less because of something the site owner has done and more because Google's systems improved their ability to recognize a real, legitimate and helpful business.

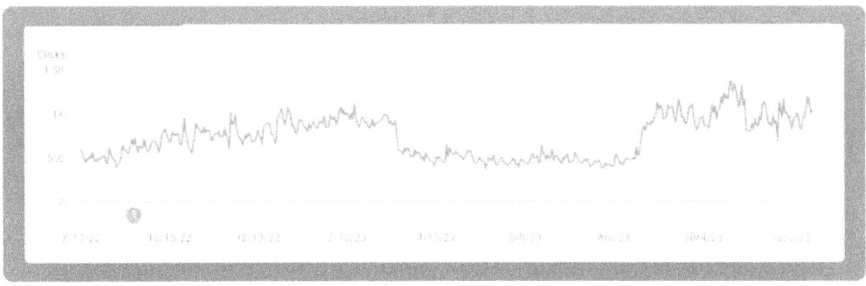

Recovery is no longer possible for all sites. There was a day when I would say that almost any website could recover following a Google update. Not today. While some sites can recover, most of the time if you are strongly impacted, the downward trend continues.

I'm going to continue to be a bit negative here before I get excited again, as it's important to explain why recovery may not be possible.

I worry most for sites that previously thrived primarily because of a good knowledge of SEO. That might sound contradictory. Let me explain.

Let's say you had a site with decent content - the type of content that a Google Quality Rater would consider medium quality - it's decently helpful, achieves the page's purpose in meeting searcher need, but doesn't really do anything to merit a high quality rating.

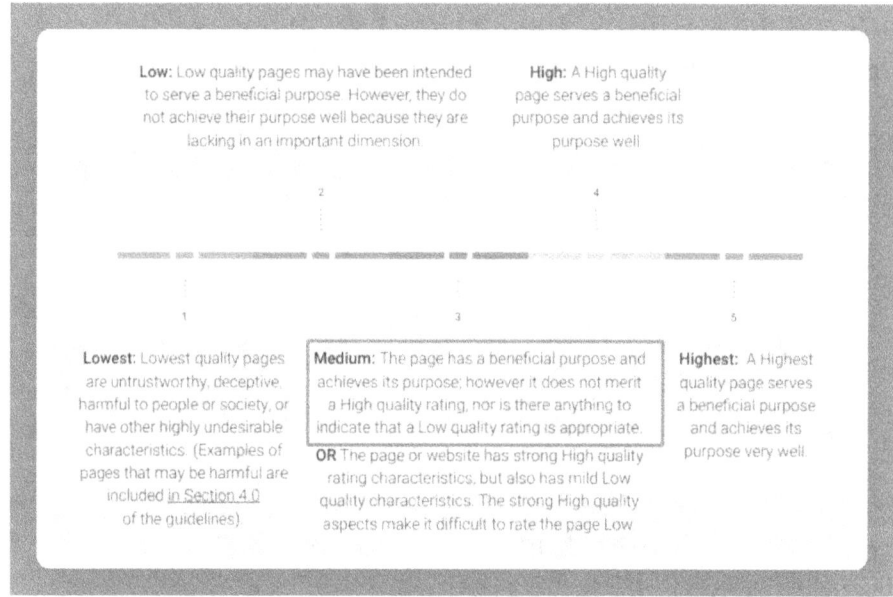

From Google's documentation on how the Search Quality Evaluator Guidelines are used[10]

---

[10] Google. November 2023. Search Quality Rater Guidelines: An Overview.

Historically, if you knew SEO, you could do many things to make that medium quality content look better to search engines than the other sites with similar medium quality content:

Good use of headings.

Keyword research including PAA (Looking at all of the People Also Ask results) research to make your content comprehensive and likely to be seen as relevant, covering all of the important information on a topic.

Keywords in title tags.

Internal links.

And oh yes, external links. Once again, how Google values links in their systems has changed significantly.

I'm not saying all of these things are worthless today. A site can gain advantages over competitors because it's technically sound, fast or well organized. You *should* be working on improving your technical SEO. But it's less and less likely these days that technical changes actually make content likely to be **significantly more helpful** than what currently exists online. Content really does need to be the top priority for most sites.

---

https://services.google.com/fh/files/misc/hsw-sqrg.pdf

There are many good, legitimate businesses that have found great success online in the past because of a knowledge of SEO. As Google's algorithms use more AI, the game changes. Instead of using PageRank (the signals that flow through links pointing to your site) as the main indication of whether content is likely to be high quality, Google now has a myriad of AI systems that attempt to do this. They've been incrementally improving these, and relying more and more on AI systems and processes for many years now.

I do not think that businesses who thrived with a knowledge of SEO and link building have now been penalized. Rather, Google is shifting more and more to a search engine that relies on deep learning, machine learning systems, and as you'll see, a complex mixture of AI systems that continue to improve upon predicting which content the searcher is likely to engage with. They learn from watching what users click on and whether they engage with it. The system is getting much harder to game.

It still *is* being gamed. There is a significant amount of spam, or in other words, content that Google doesn't want to rank, that is able to rank well. We'll discuss this as well. Perhaps I am being overly optimistic, but I suspect that Google's AI systems, including their AI brain called SpamBrain are learning and will soon be able to recognize and demote the wave of AI generated spam that is flooding the search results as I write this book.

I'll share with you how we can learn from this spam!

At the end of this book, I share some thoughts on where the future of marketing online is headed. AI has not only changed how Google ranks results, but is poised to make a significant change in how the world gets and uses information online. While I am greatly concerned about the job loss that I predict will happen for many who publish online, I believe that overall, there are more good opportunities out there. I'll share a few areas where I think there is great potential for success.

For all of us who are reading this book I believe we are on the cusp of an age where there is incredible opportunity for those who understand AI, machine learning and especially, how to get the most out of large language model tools like Gemini and ChatGPT.

About Marie

My name is Marie Haynes. In 2008 I was a veterinarian with a side hobby of learning more about how Google's search engine rankings worked. This hobby turned into an obsession in not only understanding what happened when an algorithm update happened, but turning that knowledge into actionable advice for the website owners who were impacted.

I got my start in SEO by helping websites that had received a manual action from Google. We don't see these nearly as often today. I experimented, as a hobby at first, and shared my successes and strategies in forums and blog posts. In 2012-13, I was often receiving several requests a day for help removing a Google manual penalty. I started a newsletter to tell people when Google had pushed out a significant change to their ranking systems. And bit by bit as I learned more about what Google wants to reward, I put it in the newsletter.

Tip: If you want to learn a topic, and become known as a source of helpful information on a topic, start a newsletter! You'll have great motivation to know everything that is important in your industry.

As I had more and more conversations with site owners strategizing on what to do following Google's algorithm changes like the infamous Panda and Penguin, eventually I started to offer paid consulting. It turns out that people like brainstorming with me about Google!

Over the years I've had so many fascinating conversations with site owners. Over time, many of the sites taking my advice[11] had success[12] in recovering. My reputation and demand for my services grew. I hired some great folks and we spent several years building an agency that helped people recover following losses due to Google algorithm updates and system changes.

Our work helped shape the industry's understanding of Google's use of E-E-A-T[13], Experience, Expertise,

---

[11] Marie Haynes. May 30, 2013. Penguin 2.0 "recoveries" – Graphs of WMT impression data. https://www.mariehaynes.com/penguin-2-0-recoveries/

[12] Marie Haynes. October 1, 2016. Penguin 4.0 Recovery Case Studies. https://www.mariehaynes.com/penguin-4-0-recovery-case-studies/

[13] Marie Haynes. Updated Jan 2023. What is E-E-A-T. https://www.mariehaynes.com/resources/eat/

Authoritativeness and Trustworthiness as a concept to describe what their algorithms strive to reward. If anything was published at all that could help us understand E-E-A-T more, my team and I studied it, had long, fun brainstorming sessions on how we could turn that knowledge into actionable advice, and then worked directly with businesses to help implement our ideas.

For a few years, many businesses that understood how E-E-A-T was recognized and rewarded could get a serious advantage in Search. Here is a case where we simply added schema, improved the site's About page, and recommended changes to important citations around the web to establish this brand's identity and showcase the authority they had in the industry.

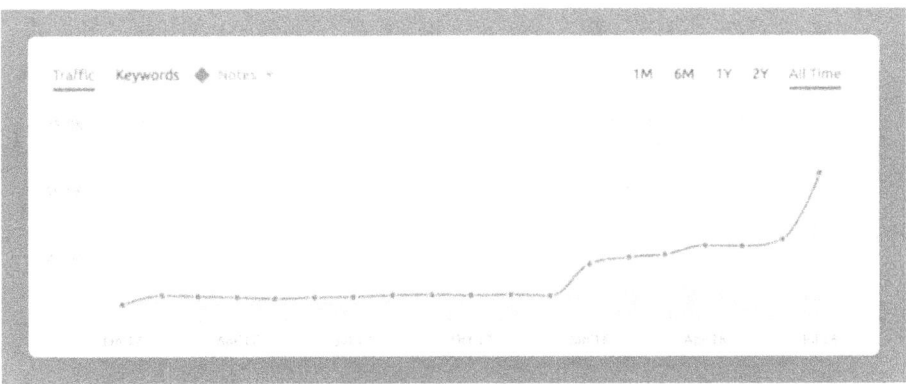

Traffic estimates from Semrush.com (I've used Semrush/Ahrefs stats in this document for sites that I do not have permission to publicly share their analytics data, or no longer have access to.)

I'm currently writing this on a beautiful desk that was sent to me by this company after this work catapulted them to top 3 rankings for most of their important high ticket keywords related to furniture.

Here's another site that took our advice, hired medical authors to co-author content on their site. It was an expensive risk for them, but it paid off. I was in their office doing live training on August 1, 2018 when Google's core update that the industry called the Medic Update rolled out.

Boy that was a fun day. Rankings were improving by the hour:

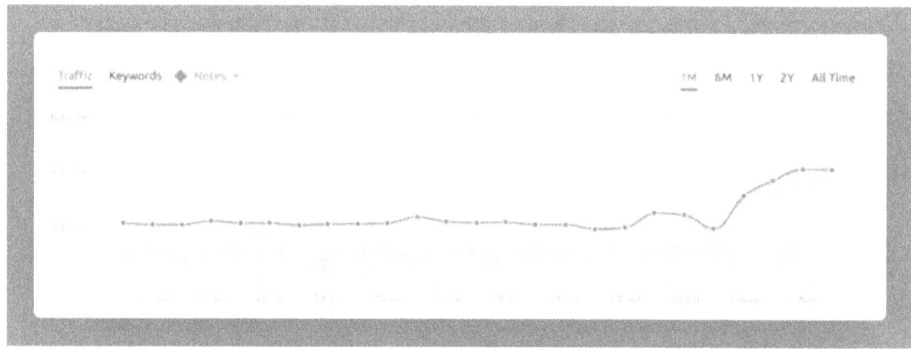

Traffic estimates from Semrush.com

For a few years, people who really understood E-E-A-T could help many businesses succeed in Search.

By 2020, my company had 12 team members on staff, 10 of which were working full time on either understanding Google's search systems, writing about that for our newsletter, or translating that into advice and recommendations in a site audit.

We had enough demand and reputation for our work in understanding Google's systems to be doing one-time exhaustive site audits as our main service.

Over the years, I have audited or in some way reviewed or consulted on thousands of websites ranging from small tiny web pages you've never heard of to some of the most recognized sites and brands on the internet. My goal with each one has been to thoroughly study what it was that Google had started to reward, and brainstorm on how they could improve with that knowledge.

When new potential clients reached out to us saying they had been impacted by a Google update, the main question they had was whether recovery was possible.

For many years, my experience was this:

If you truly have an authentic business with an audience, recovery is possible.

To some extent that is still true today...but it is much harder to recover a heavily impacted site now. Unless you legitimately have an existing audience that seeks you out, it is quite difficult to rank. It's not enough to just have good information. You need to be *known* as a source of that information.

In the past, provided you weren't a blackhat trying to manipulate Google, almost any site that put in the work that we recommended had a good chance of recovery. "The work" was often extensive. Our reports and recommendations were filled with 120+ pages with advice on things like improving Google's understanding of your E-A-T (now E-E-A-T with an extra E for experience) via schema use, on-page verbiage and acquisition of good links.

My favourite part of our reports has always been the section we called, "Page Comparisons." We had our most junior employees do this section so as not to be biased with prior learned SEO knowledge of what makes a page likely to be good and helpful. Their goal was to say, not as an SEO, but as a human searcher, why a page might be seen as more or less helpful.

It turns out that this is quite similar to how a Google quality rater rates a page.

> 10.1 Instructions for Rating Page Quality Tasks
>
> **The Page Quality task page is broken up into several parts:**
>
> 1. Some initial questions about the task landing page.
> 2. A "PQ grid" to record your observations about PQ characteristics of the landing page.
> 3. The Overall PQ rating slider which records your Overall PQ rating.
> 4. A comment box to explain your rating.

From Google's Search Quality Rater Evaluator Guidelines[14]

We'll soon see how this is important as the quality raters labels help Google's machine learning systems determine

---

[14] Google. November 16, 2023. General Guidelines (Quality Rater Guidelines). https://static.googleusercontent.com/media/guidelines.raterhub.com/en//searchqualityevaluatorguidelines.pdf

whether they are doing a good job, and provide them with examples of helpful or unhelpful results. They raters use a grid in which they jot down observations which essentially can tell Google's systems the *characteristics* that make that page helpful/unhelpful. Then, machine learning systems use that information to create or improve upon algorithms built to rank pages that the searcher is going to find helpful.

It's likely far more complicated than I have explained. What we know is that Google takes loads of signals and uses them across multiple AI systems to continually get better and better at producing helpful results.

When doing site audits, my team would navigate through the site we were reviewing and also through the sites of the competitors Google started to prefer. They were instructed to put themselves in the shoes of a searcher. Many hours were spent producing side by side screenshots showing how competitors that Google liked did a better job at meeting searcher needs, and giving our thoughts on how they could improve to do better.

Perhaps they've got a table of contents to get a searcher to their answer faster. Maybe they've got a helpful image, and a video. Or better references to support their claims. Or a more modern and trustworthy design. Often competitors would get the searcher to their answer faster, or perhaps be better known for the topic, so people would be more likely to want to engage with them.

The most useful thing you can do to determine how to improve is to look at what Google is ranking now. Be substantially better than that! Be a resource searchers will choose to engage with and then, find incredibly helpful.

The problem is, it is often hard to know how to do that. Especially if you are looking at your content like an SEO rather than a searcher.

Our reports also included a standard technical audit, improvements for core web vital improvements, internal link recommendations and more.

In most cases, what happened after we delivered our report was that the site owners would implement the changes that they thought they hired us for - the "SEO changes" that they could make, or hand off to a developer to make.

But often they would not make the drastic content changes we suggested.

This makes sense as the changes needed to truly improve can be expensive and time consuming, and sometimes are not even possible. If you have thousands of pages of content that is all mediocre, improving those to all be truly better and more helpful than what competitors are offering is no simple task.

For a while, improving everything you could in terms of technical SEO had good potential to help sites.

But over time, as Google develops more and more ways to determine which content and websites searchers are finding helpful, technical changes are less and less likely to provide significant return. One exception may be improving site hierarchy to help improve topical authority. We'll talk more about that shortly.

Despite our urgency in our reports to say that great changes in content quality and helpfulness were needed, we found that the Page Comparisons section of our report was rarely seriously acted upon.

Why?

It's because we were giving site owners recommendations that would require entire changes to their business model, often costly changes.

Google's documentation is very clear on what it is that they say users consider to be helpful content. Note: These are not necessarily specific things that Google's system checks. Rather, they are the types of things that searchers like. And *that's* what the ranking systems are built to produce.

> - Does the content provide original information, reporting, research, or analysis?
>
> - Does the content provide insightful analysis or interesting information that is beyond the obvious?
> - If the content draws on other sources, does it avoid simply copying or rewriting those sources, and instead provide substantial additional value and originality?
>
> - Is this the sort of page you'd want to bookmark, share with a friend, or recommend?
> - Would you expect to see this content in or referenced by a printed magazine, encyclopedia, or book?
> - Does the content provide substantial value when compared to other pages in search results?
>
> - Do you have an existing or intended audience for your business or site that would find the content useful if they came directly to you?
> - Does your content clearly demonstrate first-hand expertise and a depth of knowledge (for example, expertise that comes from having actually used a product or service, or visiting a place)?

A few of the suggestions Google has given us to consider when we assess our content[15].

You cannot produce original, insightful content that truly demonstrates experience and trustworthiness by outsourcing all of your writing to a copywriter and publishing with minimal editing and no added insight. But for years, many businesses thrived on this model!

You can't add truly helpful graphics, unique images and video without extensive effort and extra cost, even if that cost is your time. **You cannot create the type of content that people find worthy of bookmarking or sharing with others without significant effort.**

---

[15] Creating helpful, reliable, people-first content. Google. https://developers.google.com/search/docs/fundamentals/creating-helpful-content Retrieved Dec 2023.

The other difficulty is that improving just a few pages is not generally enough for recovery. Changes need to be made sitewide in many cases to convince Google's search systems that your site is among the most helpful sites to put in front of searchers. Otherwise, why should they spend time and money crawling your content that they're rarely likely to show to people?

It was difficult for us to provide evidence to convince the business that they'd get ROI by implementing the improvements we had suggested. And for many businesses the things we were asking the site owner to do to improve quality were simply not possible without a wild change in business practices.

By 2022 I had a serious problem in my business. We understood *why* most sites were impacted by changes to Google's systems. But we could no longer boast that most of the sites that came to us for help would be able to recover.

Increasingly, the pages that ranked better in an update really *were* pages that deserved to rank because users would find them a helpful result, and not because they had better SEO than competitors. The only fix is to **be a substantially better result**. And often that was not possible as the better result was perhaps an official organization, a real life business with real world customers, or a giant authority in the industry. Even if you did have better content, it would be hard to convince users to get that content on your site rather than the known authorities. These are not things that are easily achievable via SEO, and certainly not tasks you could hand off to a developer or employee to simply implement.

While we were still seeing some recoveries amongst our clients in 2022, the vast majority of reports that we sent out essentially concluded that recovery was either not possible or would take gargantuan effort and cost with no guarantee of success.

Consulting slowly morphed into grief counseling as one site owner after the other was told that they likely would not have success if they kept doing what they were doing. And few had the resources or drive to attempt creating truly original and helpful content.

I no longer have an agency. It was a thoroughly enjoyable time of my life and I am grateful for the wonderful team I was able to learn alongside.

We disbanded MHC in 2022. I returned to solo consulting. I poured myself into understanding more and more about how to help the many businesses that reached out to me, suffering following a change to Google's systems.

There is still good reason for much of what we do in the name of SEO. However, my hope is that this book challenges some of the beliefs you hold on what makes a website and its content look good to Google.

The secret is **to have a website and content that *people* seek out and click on.** That usually means having an audience that recognizes you as a go-to source on your topic. More importantly than that, it means **understanding what that audience's needs are.**

Many of the sites impacted by recent Google updates were created for Google first, rather than for an audience of people who truly are hungry to engage with you. If this is the case for you, it is possible that you will not recover. I will help you decide if that is you, and if so, help you get inspired on what to do next. There are so many opportunities opening up!

Do not despair though. I still see cases of recovery. Sometimes it happens after a site owner has worked very hard to improve the helpfulness of their content. And sometimes sites recover by doing nothing at all! I have seen several cases like this with recent updates - all likely related to Google doing more to recognize and reward real-world experience. Often now, a seemingly poorly optimized website can outrank one that looks perfect to an SEO if it really is helpful content.

What I am most excited about is what Google calls "hidden gems". A section of this book is dedicated to what I suspect you might be - a hidden gem. We will look at the future and speculate at what it will take to be found online as the world uses more and more AI to find the answers to their questions.

Part 1: AI has changed how Search works

Much of the SEO advice you will see online today is borne from shared community wisdom that was learned about Search in the days before Google was actively using AI. So much of what many of us do as SEOs and treat as standard practice is based on a search engine that was a list of heuristics - handwritten rules programmed by humans. So much has changed.

For example, let's say you are tasked with creating a new article for the website you are working on. You'll likely start with keyword research because we know that in order to appear relevant to a search engine, you need to write content that covers a topic thoroughly and uses keywords that are semantically related to your topic.

So much of the content that we have on the web today is borne from a process that looks like this:

- Do keyword research to see what your competitors have written.
- Create content that's similar but perhaps a little bit better, or more comprehensive than theirs.
- Do keyword research to see what other people have covered, but you have not included.
- Create content that covers that stuff too.
- Do People Also Ask research to find related questions to cover so that we can write content that looks even

- more relevant and comprehensive to search engines.
- Create more content to answer those questions even though Google already has content to answer them.

Nothing in that process is causing us to create content that truly is original, insightful, and **substantially more helpful than what exists online**.

Yet, that is what Google wants to reward!

An SEO agency will often spend many hours each month improving the technical SEO of a site, improving the internal link structure, or perhaps getting external links and mentions. These are all things that can possibly help a webpage to look better to a search engine. They are not bad things to do and some of them have the potential to help a site improve. But again, those things are unlikely to make the content on a page **substantially more helpful to searchers,** which is, once again, what Google wants to reward.

I want to be clear here. **I'm not saying that technical SEO is dead.** There are benefits to be had by having a technically sound, fast site that search engines can easily navigate and understand, especially if you have a large site. Schema can still do wonders when it comes to helping Google understand your business and its E-E-A-T, especially a new one. There are some verticals where technical improvements will give you enough advantage to improve rankings to some degree.

There is one thing that makes content more helpful.

Are you ready for this deep, insightful secret?

Here it is…

The secret to having content that is likely to be considered by Google as more helpful than others' is to have content that users are finding helpful.

A mindset shift is needed for SEOs

For more than a decade now, my main source of income has come from advising businesses how to improve their search presence.

I have pored over every word Google has published that talks about what it is that they want to reward and have produced pages and pages of checklists, training documents and advice.

I had one goal: **Help people understand what it is that Google rewards, and help them become that result.**

Do you see the paradox that is hidden in that statement? The more I think about it, it's laughable!

I didn't realize the whole time that while I was preaching on creating **People-first content**, as Google now calls it, much of what I was doing was geared far more towards **satisfying Google than searchers**.

Other SEOs are catching on to this mindset as well now. What users do on our websites matters immensely. The actions of users shape Google's rankings dramatically.

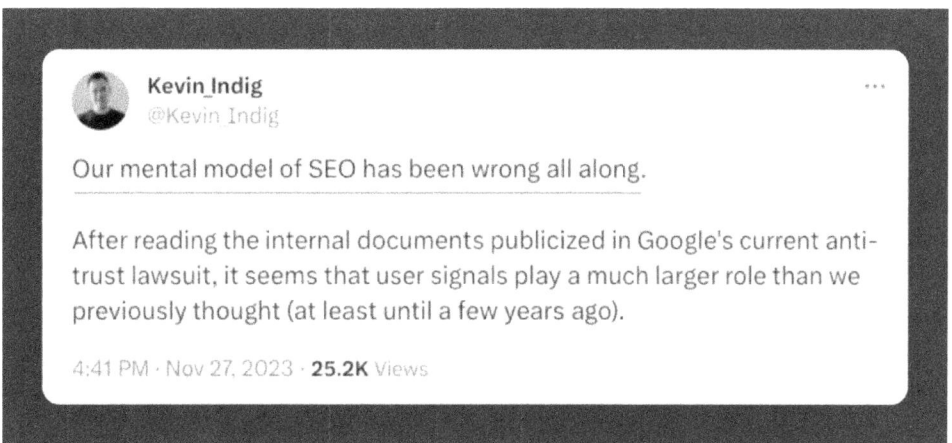

I have historically treated Google's guidance on creating helpful content as a checklist of things we could look to for improvement. Have an author bio? Check. Good descriptive heading? Check. Demonstrating experience? Information gain? Another check.

My first book on creating helpful content[16] takes you through multiple checklists like this. You *can* see improvement by working through these checklists. Actually, I know this as I commonly will have people reach out to me to tell me that

---

[16] Creating Helpful Content. Marie Haynes. 2023.
https://mariehaynes.com/product/creating-helpful-content-workbook/

they have implemented changes based on the checklists and have been seeing improvements.

But, it turns out what Google gave us was not a list of criteria to be analyzed as a checklist!

I realize now that what Google was telling us was, **Our systems are built to reward the types of things that people tend to find helpful and reliable. And if you want to know what that is, here are some ideas.** It's not a checklist, but rather, a list of the **types of things that searchers tend to like**. The algorithm is built to reward what it is that searchers like.

An author bio isn't a ranking factor, but, in many verticals, demonstrating the experience of your authors is something that users like. Core web vitals, metrics used to measure load time and other similar things, used to be a score we'd aim to get...but really, the reason we work to improve on core web vital scores is because users tend to like pages that load fast and don't jump around. It's not like Google has a checklist or a scorecard when it comes to the quality of every page. Google doesn't *know* exactly what your content is or whether it is high quality. As we discussed earlier, search is a complex AI driven system that is **trying to predict what searchers are going to find helpful**.

Here are the full list of "ideas" Google gives us to help us understand what searchers might find helpful:

Content and quality questions

- Does the content provide original information, reporting, research, or analysis?
- Does the content provide a substantial, complete, or comprehensive description of the topic?
- Does the content provide insightful analysis or interesting information that is beyond the obvious?
- If the content draws on other sources, does it avoid simply copying or rewriting those sources, and instead provide substantial additional value and originality?
- Does the main heading or page title provide a descriptive, helpful summary of the content?
- Does the main heading or page title avoid exaggerating or being shocking in nature?
- Is this the sort of page you'd want to bookmark, share with a friend, or recommend?
- Would you expect to see this content in or referenced by a printed magazine, encyclopedia, or book?
- Does the content provide substantial value when compared to other pages in search results?
- Does the content have any spelling or stylistic issues?
- Is the content produced well, or does it appear sloppy or hastily produced?
- Is the content mass-produced by or outsourced to a large number of creators, or spread across a large network of sites, so that individual pages or sites don't get as much attention or care?

Expertise questions

- Does the content present information in a way that makes you want to trust it, such as clear sourcing, evidence of the expertise involved, background about the author or the site that publishes it, such as through links to an author page or a site's About page?
- If someone researched the site producing the content, would they come away with an impression that it is well-trusted or widely-recognized as an authority on its topic?
- Is this content written or reviewed by an expert or enthusiast who demonstrably knows the topic well?
- Does the content have any easily-verified factual errors?

Provide a great page experience

Google's core ranking systems look to reward content that provides a good page experience. Site owners seeking to be successful with our systems should not focus on only one or two aspects of page experience. Instead, check if you're providing an overall great page experience across many aspects. For more advice, see our page, Understanding page experience in Google Search results.

Answering yes to the questions below means you're probably on track in providing a good page experience:

- Do pages have good Core Web Vitals?
- Are pages served in a secure fashion?
- Does content display well for mobile devices when viewed on them?
- Does the content lack an excessive amount of ads that distract from or interfere with the main content?
- Do pages lack intrusive interstitials?
- How easily can visitors navigate to or locate the main content of your pages?
- Is the page designed so visitors can easily distinguish the main content from other content on your page

Focus on people-first content

People-first content means content that's created primarily for people, and not to manipulate search engine rankings. How can you evaluate if you're creating people-first content? Answering yes to the questions below means you're probably on the right track with a people-first approach:

- Do you have an existing or intended audience for your business or site that would find the content useful if they came directly to you?
- Does your content clearly demonstrate first-hand expertise and a depth of knowledge (for example, expertise that comes from having actually used a product or service, or visiting a place)?
- Does your site have a primary purpose or focus?
- After reading your content, will someone leave feeling they've learned enough about a topic to help achieve their goal?
- Will someone reading your content leave feeling like they've had a satisfying experience?

> **Avoid creating search engine-first content**
>
> We recommend that you focus on creating people-first content to be successful with Google Search, rather than search engine-first content made primarily to gain search engine rankings. Answering yes to some or all of the questions below is a warning sign that you should reevaluate how you're creating content:
>
> - Is the content primarily made to attract visits from search engines?
> - Are you producing lots of content on many different topics in hopes that some of it might perform well in search results?
> - Are you using extensive automation to produce content on many topics?
> - Are you mainly summarizing what others have to say without adding much value?
> - Are you writing about things simply because they seem trending and not because you'd write about them otherwise for your existing audience?
> - Does your content leave readers feeling like they need to search again to get better information from other sources?
> - Are you writing to a particular word count because you've heard or read that Google has a preferred word count? (No, we don't.)
> - Did you decide to enter some niche topic area without any real expertise, but instead mainly because you thought you'd get search traffic?
> - Does your content promise to answer a question that actually has no answer, such as suggesting there's a release date for a product, movie, or TV show when one isn't confirmed?
> - Are you changing the date of pages to make them seem fresh when the content has not substantially changed?
> - Are you adding a lot of new content or removing a lot of older content primarily because you believe it will help your search rankings overall by somehow making your site seem "fresh?" (No, it won't)

In the past I've taught on looking at these ideals one by one for inspiration on how you can improve your site. I still think there is great value in doing this.

But, now I realize I was missing the main point. I have been thinking about helpful content **like an SEO**.

If you are truly creating People-First content, you will already be aligned with Google's helpful content recommendations.

I had it the wrong way around.

If you know what your audience's needs are, and know the questions that they have, and you create content that answers those questions you are on your way to creating the type of People-First Content Google wants to reward.

People first content is:

- **Usually created by people with real world experience on a topic**. A store that sells a product to real customers is more likely to produce helpful content advising people on that product. A person who advises professionally on a topic, is more likely to have fresh content that understands the current needs of that audience.

    There is an exception to this: Sometimes authority can trump experience. We see this when a website like Forbes is ranking for "BBQ reviews". In this case, Forbes is likely seen as a place that users trust for its overall authority in journalism. It's got sufficient EEAT to be considered a trustworthy answer for this query. And as long as searchers are indicating they are satisfied, it will continue to rank. (I think this will change though as we learn to create truly helpful content. We should start to see more truly helpful content from topic experts recommended.)
- **Content that provides real value to searchers.**
- **Written clearly and concisely in a manner that is easy to understand.**
- **Original and insightful.**

But how does Google determine this? In the next section we'll talk about something that has been mostly unknown to SEOs until just recently - just how much Google uses user engagement signals. It turns out that Google knows what it is that's helpful to people because **signals from every single interaction that happens in search are fed back into machine learning systems with one goal in mind - for the systems to learn how to best work together to create present the searcher with information that they are most likely to find helpful.**

Navboost: Google's use of user engagement signals

The United States' Department of Justice is currently in a legal case with Google regarding monopolization. A large number of trial exhibits[17] have been published that tell us many things about how Google's ranking systems work.

I think you will be as shocked as I was when I realized just how much user engagement signals such as clicks, scrolls, mouse hovers and other metrics are used as signals that

---

[17] U.S. and Plaintiff States v. Google LLC [2020] - Trial Exhibits. Antitrust Division - US Department of Justice. November 2023.
https://www.justice.gov/atr/us-and-plaintiff-states-v-google-llc-2020-trial-exhibits

indicate whether or not a search has been helpful. A system called Navboost stores these signals so that Google's systems can learn from them.

They also talk about something they refer to as IS - Information Satisfaction signals, gleaned from the work of the quality raters. These signals are all used in machine learning systems to help Google improve their ability to predict which websites people are likely to find helpful. They have been for many years now.

Here is information from the exhibit in the DOJ vs Google trial called, Life of a Click[18].

> we may use "clicks" as a stand-in for "user-interactions" in some places user-interactions include clicks, attention on a result, swipes on carousels and entering a new query

These interaction signals are used in multiple machine learning (AI) systems with names like RankBrain, DeepRank, and RankEmbed, all vitally important to search.

---

[18] Trial Exhibit-UPX0004: U.S. and Plaintiff States v. Google LLC. May 15, 2017. https://www.justice.gov/d9/2023-11/417508.pdf

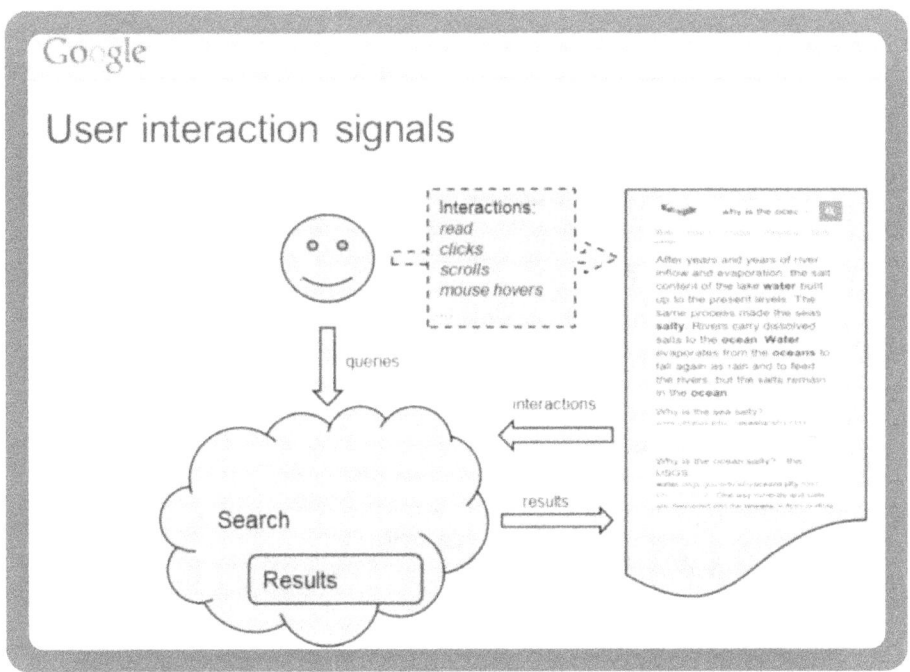

From the Life of a Click presentation in the DOJ trial exhibits. This diagram shows that interactions like reads, clicks, scrolls, mouse hovers and more are fed back into the system to improve Search results.

Interactions can include reads, clicks, scrolls, mouse hovers and more as people use Google search. These are all signals that can be used across multiple AI systems as signals that might indicate whether a search has been satisfied.

Together these systems are used to refine Google's results.

Here are a few excerpts from the transcript where Google's Pandu Nayak was being questioned about how the algorithm works.

So we were talking about how Google goes from one circle to the other, as part of your direct. Google uses what you've called core algorithms to bring that down to a set of about 200 documents, right?

A. Several hundred, yes.

Q. Several hundred. And I'm just going to write "core algorithm," because I'm probably going to use that.

And those algorithms give the documents initial rankings or scores, right?

A. Yes.

Q. And an application of BERT, when BERT is used for ranking, is DeepRank, right?

A. Yes.

Q. And DeepRank is trained on user data?

A. Yes, it is.

Q. So let's start with RankBrain. RankBrain looks at the top 20 or 30 documents and may adjust their initial score; is that right?

A. That is correct.

```
                                                               6432
    Q.  RankBrain is trained on queries across all languages
and locales Google operates in?
    A.  I think so, yes.
    Q.  And then it's fine-tuned on IS data?
    A.  That is correct.
    Q.  But it is not possible to train RankBrain on only
human rater data, right?
    A.  No, you can't.
    Q.  And each time RankBrain is retrained, it is with fresh
data, right?
    A.  It's with -- yes, with new data, yeah.
    Q.  And for years, RankBrain was trained on 13 months
worth of click and query data; is that right?
    A.  I think initially it started with the same amount as
navboost, yes.
```

We go through much more of this testimony in (possibly excruciating) detail in the course.

I think the SEO community is due for a radical mindset shift in understanding what is and isn't important when it comes to ranking. I'd like to share with you my current understanding of how ranking works.

The goal here is not to teach you *exactly how* ranking works, but rather, to convince you that bit by bit, Google is using AI to move ever so slowly, incrementally closer to being a search engine that understands what a person needs and which content they are likely to find the most helpful to meet that need.

I believe recent advancements with Gemini will speed these advancements up.

If you can grasp what I'm trying to say here, it will be easier to accept that the algo is built to reward content that searchers are likely to find helpful, and that creating helpful, people-first content is by far the most important "ranking factor" if such a thing even exists.

My understanding of how ranking works in 2024:

Google uses a complex system of hundreds of algorithms to rank search results.

- **The initial ranking of search results is determined by a set of "core algorithms"** that Google uses to find content from its index that is likely to be relevant to a search. We can discuss these in more detail, but really it's understanding the re-ranking step that will be the difference maker.

  - The hundreds of results returned by the core ranking systems are **narrowed down to the top 20-30 pages** that are most likely to help a searcher.

- **RankBrain** - a machine learning (AI) system that learns from user engagement and other signals, re-ranks those top 20-30 results. RankBrain uses user engagement signals - clicks, hovers, scrolls and more to rank results. Then, the Information Satisfaction data that come from the feedback of human search quality raters are used to fine-tune those results. These ratings and notes are made based on learning about quality from a publicly available document called Google's Quality Rater Guidelines[19].

    To simplify things further:

---

[19] Google's Search Quality Evaluator Guidelines PDF. Google. November 16, 2023.
https://static.googleusercontent.com/media/guidelines.raterhub.com/en//searchqualityevaluatorguidelines.pdf

Each time a query is searched, Google finds hundreds of documents that are likely to be relevant. Then, they take the top 20-30 of those documents and use a complex mixture of AI systems to re-rank them according to the machine learning systems' predictions of which are likely to be the most helpful.

If you are doing SEO like we did in 2008, some of what you do may help you in Google's traditional ranking algorithms. But once you have a site that consistently is able to rank in the top few hundred results, what matters is how the AI systems, including RankBrain view your site.

Hopefully by this point I have not caused too much confusion. It has taken me over a year to be able to understand and explain this topic, and there is much more to learn still.

I have written significantly more on what we have learned from the DOJ trial exhibits. In the course that goes along with this book you'll find:

- The full list of DOJ slides for you to review yourself

- The full Pandu Nayak testimony where he discusses how RankBrain, DeepRank, Navboost, Information Satisfaction signals like clicks, hovers and scrolls, and the quality raters.

And AI assistants like this one that I created with loads of papers, the DOJ testimony and more in its knowledge base.

Understand more about Search
Chat with the information in the DOJ trial against Google to learn more about how AI has changed search
By Marie Haynes Consulting Inc.

You
what algorithm components or AI systems were discussed in the trial

Understand more about Search
The trial discussed several algorithm components and AI systems used by Google, as outlined in the documents:

1. **Core Algorithms and Deep Learning Systems**: Google's search relies on several hundred core algorithms, termed "traditional systems," to rank results. Deep learning systems are then used to adjust these scores. Some of the deep learning systems mentioned include:
    - **RankEmbed**: This system, which includes RankEmbed BERT, is used for retrieving documents. It is trained on click and query data and fine-tuned using human Informational Satisfaction (IS) rater data. RankEmbed supplements the traditional information retrieval system and requires continual retraining.
    - **Navboost and Glue**: Navboost is employed after the initial retrieval of results to further rank web results. Glue, a variation of Navboost, determines which Search Engine Results Page (SERP) features should be displayed. Both Navboost and Glue utilize user engagement signals like clicks, scrolls, and mouse hovers.
    - **RankBrain and DeepRank**: These are two of the three deep learning models used by Google. RankBrain adjusts the scores of the top 20-30 documents based on queries and IS data, while DeepRank, a language model derived from BERT, understands language and context for ranking purposes. DeepRank is also trained on user interactions but requires human quality raters for comprehensive understanding.

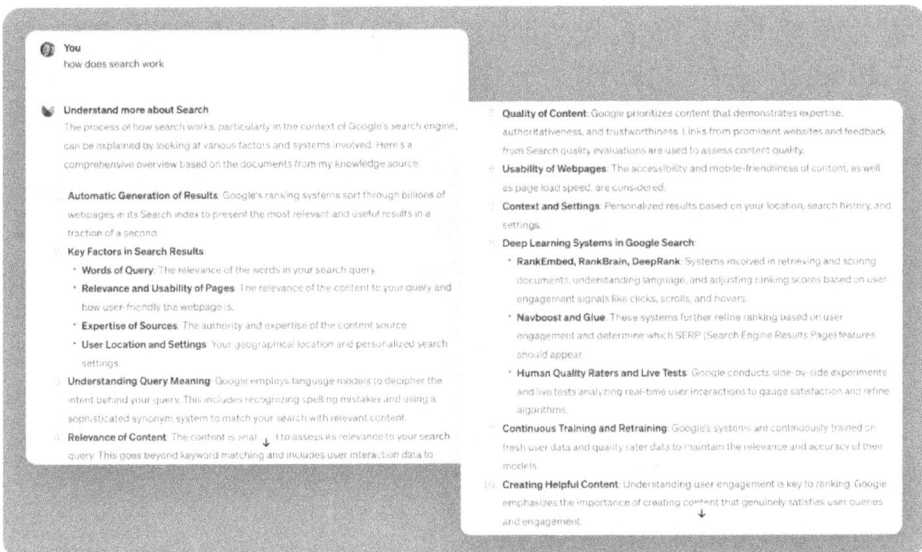

I expect that we will see more helpful writing from our industry soon as well as more industry leaders and folks in the trenches dig into these newly available DOJ documents.

How does this information change how we create content on our websites?

We can do one of two things now that we understand that Google's search results have changed over the years and rely heavily on user engagement signals and AI to determine how to rank results.

1) We can try to reverse engineer how Google determines what is relevant and what is likely to align with the systems that determine helpfulness.

2) We can keep this knowledge in mind as we focus primarily on helping our audience.

Given how rapidly Google's systems change as they develop new technology and as their systems continue to learn, I'd encourage you to focus on number 2. However, we can certainly do more to understand what it is that people find engaging and improve in this area.

You made it this far!

Hopefully by this point I have convinced you that Google's systems once were gameable by those with good knowledge of SEO, but the more Google uses and develops their AI systems, the less it is that SEO is what makes content rank. Rather, it's overall helpfulness.

Links. How Google values them has changed.

Let's go back to 2008. I was a veterinarian who had created a hobby website where people could ask me veterinary advice. I answered many commonly asked veterinary questions for free and published them on my site. Despite me having good, helpful content, It was getting a measly 30 visitors or so per day.

So I started learning about SEO. Most of my learning came from forum discussions. One thing was pretty clear in 2008. You could do all sorts of things to improve the technical SEO of your website, but if you wanted to rank, you needed links.

I changed my signature in all of my forum profiles to include a link anchored with the words, "online veterinary advice". I created an account at Ezine articles and published short, quickly written articles on vague veterinary topics. My author bio, once again, advised that you could ask a vet online. My best link building success was when I built a calculator you could use to determine whether your dog ate enough chocolate to warrant an emergency vet visit.

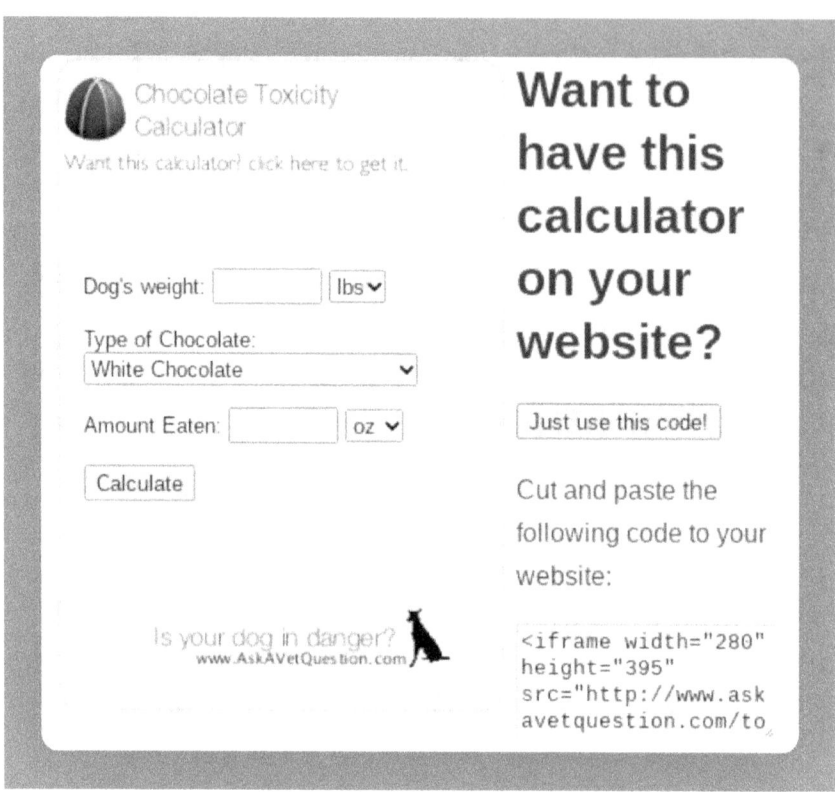

That code you could use to embed this calculator on your site contained a link inviting you to try the calculator for yourself and get online veterinary advice. Many veterinary clinics and even authoritative sites linked to that page because it was helpful.

That last type of link is the type we should still be aiming for - not ones that require site owners to link back with anchor text that is scripted with intent to manipulate rankings, but rather, links that are gained because people found your content, you, or your business, helpful enough to recommend to others.

Are links still used in Google's ranking systems?

Yes. Google's guide to their ranking systems[20] tells us that PageRank, which is the measure of a site's link quality, was one of their core ranking systems when Google first launched. It has "evolved a lot since then," but is still used.

> **Link analysis systems and PageRank**
>
> We have various systems that understand how pages link to each other as a way to determine what pages are about and which might be most helpful in response to a query. Among these is PageRank, one of our core ranking systems used when Google first launched. Those curious can learn more by reading the original PageRank research paper and patent. How PageRank works has evolved a lot since then, and it continues to be part of our core ranking systems.

Links were at one time the primary signal used in Google's calculations. Today, they use many signals.

In 2016, Google employee Andrey Lipattsev told us that links were among the top 3 ranking signals. The other two were content and RankBrain[21]. This has changed.

I was in the audience at the Search Conference Pubcon in September 2023 when Google employee Gary Illyes was

---

[20] Google Search Central blog. A guide to Google Search ranking systems. https://developers.google.com/search/docs/appearance/ranking-systems-guide

[21] Search Engine Roundtable. Barry Schwartz. Google: The Top Three Ranking Factors Are Content, Links & RankBrain. March 2016. https://www.seroundtable.com/google-top-three-ranking-factors-21827.html

questioned by Jennifer Slegg. Here is the picture I took from my front row seat.

Gary said that while links remain important, SEO's often overestimate their importance. "It is possible to rank without links," he said, "Content is the #1 factor."

Jennifer asked, "Are links still one of the most important ranking factors?"

His response (I've bolded the parts I thought were most important.)

*"I think **they are important** but I do think that people are overestimating the importance of links. **It hasn't been top 3 for some time already.** "*

This doesn't mean that all links are ignored by Google's systems.

My thoughts on links

Over the years I have thoroughly studied Google's use of links, and in particular, SEO's abuse of links to manipulate rankings.

I removed hundreds of Google manual actions that came to sites who had abused link building. This helped me understand what was previously working, and what Google was looking to combat. Eventually I had an entire manual actions division in my company. We trained every team member to be able to discern how likely it was that a link was created for SEO purposes or one that really was a recommendation and a vote for our client's site.

The team came up with creative ways to train new members including a Who wants to be a Links-ionaire game the whole team would play.

We spent hours debating what Google's systems would and wouldn't consider worth counting in their ranking calculations and then brainstorming on strategies for disavowing links, removing manual actions, and in some cases, recovering from algorithmic link related suppressions.

In 2012, the links that were getting sites manual actions from Google were low quality directory and article links. By 2020, link audits were brutal. We had case after case of sites that had learned how to create "white hat" links and had a copious number of mentions from authoritative and well known sites. It was often difficult to determine which links were created for SEO purposes and which were naturally earned. This was because, by this time, link builders had become very good at making links "look natural" to Google's systems in ways that really did help move the needle.

Why does Google put effort into dishing out manual actions? It's not common to get a manual action for unnatural links these days because Google's algorithms are quite good at determining which links to count and which to ignore. They don't need to manually discount links for many sites.

When they do, it's generally for sophisticated link building schemes that make it very difficult for Google's systems to know what to pay attention to and what to ignore.

Google gives manual actions because **links still matter.** We see far fewer of them today, but they do still occur. My thought is that if Google needs to manually discount links pointing to sites, then it means that there are situations where links are helping a site.

I believe that some links matter, but many of the links that used to be counted as positive signals by Google are ignored now. Much of what is done in the name of link building today is likely a waste of money. Google has been training their machine learning systems to understand which links are worth paying attention to for many years now.

PageRank is a **signal** determined by math that estimates the quality of links pointing to a page. Years ago this **was one of the strongest signals** Google had to help them approximate quality. A page that had high quality links pointing to it was very likely to be a high quality page - especially if those links came from authoritative places. Today, links are just **one of the many signals** that Google can use to predict which content is likely to be helpful and reliable.

New information from Google's API docs "leak"

I'm about to publish this book and the SEO world is abuzz with news of a ["leak" of Google documentation](). It's not actually a leak. This documentation for API calls to Google's Content Warehouse has been publicly available on Github since 2022.

The SEO world has been finding all sorts of interesting things amongst the attributes listed in these files. While they don't tell us exactly how Google's systems are working, they tell us a lot of information about what is stored in terms of PageRank.

Some of the attributes include: pagerankWeight, anchor, isLocal and much more.

I expect we will see some excellent analysis that helps us understand more about how Google's systems use links. Or, possibly how the systems *used to use* links.

Personally, I believe that Google's breakthroughs in both technology and improving the efficiency of their AI models with [Gemini 1.5]()'s new architecture have brought them to a place where they have significantly more computational power. This allows their machine learning systems to do more, and to use more signals, with PageRank being one of them, as they work to predict what a searcher will find helpful.

Where does that leave us in terms of understanding links?

Let me share my current thoughts on how links are used in Google's systems. Then, I'll help you determine whether you should be focusing on link building.

Here are my current thoughts on links

- **Links help Google discover new content you have published.** This is not a problem for a well-crawled site that people are using and finding helpful, especially one with good internal linking. If you're new though, links from places that matter can help you get content discovered. This is one of the reasons why link building is a crucial component of most blackhat SEO campaigns. If you don't legitimately have an audience actively engaging with your site, then you'll need links to get Google's attention on your content.
- **Links help Google understand what topics you are known for.** If you are trying to become known for your topics, then getting others known for your topics to link to you, can help improve your chances of being recommended for this topic. You want to aim for true recommendations - the type of link that Google's systems are likely to find worthy of including in their calculations. Being known for your topic is so important.
- **Links help E-E-A-T.** Links that truly represent a recommendation or a positive mention of your business or your content contribute to the signals in

the world that make up the concept of E-E-A-T for your brand and help determine what you are known for.

Remember Larry Page's dream? The idea that was given to him was that you could understand the information on the web by just downloading the links.

In the course, we discuss links in more detail and brainstorm on how you can get more links that are likely to send good signals to Google that people truly are recommending you and finding your content helpful.

The mismatch between black hat SEOs who have success building links and white hats who do not

Over the years I have had a lot of conversations brainstorming over what works and what doesn't in terms of links. Some websites have had budgets of tens of thousands per month just to build links in the name of PR (public relations.) In reality, once you've looked at thousands or perhaps millions of links as I have, it gets easier to spot the patterns of links that exist for SEO versus links that really do represent people talking about your business.

If I can see those patterns, then imagine the patterns the machine learning systems that have access to so much data can see.

I have preached for years now that Google is good at ignoring unnatural links because that's what Google's documentation says. And also that's what my experience and the experience of most sites that I work with has been. I've worked with quite a few site owners who have tried so many different ways to build links with no success.

Yet at the same time, I know plenty of people who are blackhat SEOs who claim that links are crucial and that it is still the main tool in their toolbox when it comes to ranking. And I believe them! (Well some of them. I think some who boast about link building are simply sneakily trying to get people to buy links from their service.)

There are some SEOs whom I have known for years who really do tell me that links are the biggest driver of rankings. These folks genuinely cannot fathom how I would conclude anything else.

After reading the Nyak testimony, an idea came to me that possibly explains how both of us could be right.

I think it's possible that links matter immensely if you are doing blackhat SEO. If you are doing people-first SEO, truly good links can help, but for different reasons.

Links are important when it comes to helping Google discover new information. It is generally not a problem for a site to get its content indexed on Google if it has content that people like. This is because Google is happily crawling and indexing the content on these sites.

For sites that rank mostly because of SEO efforts, more needs to be done to get crawlers to visit. Links are needed.

If you have a legitimate business that people seek out and find useful you likely will find that it's not hard to get Google to find your content via regular site crawls. For me, if I publish a new blog post, it's generally in Google's index within a few hours. For some of my clients it's very fast.

Many sites lately have been struggling to get Google to index content. If this is you, I would take this as a sign that quality improvements may be needed.

So, let's say I have a spam site. A spam site is a site that contains content that looks good to Google's algorithms and ranks well in their systems, but that really is not what they want their systems to reward.

Right now with AI's ability to create content, it is still possible for manipulative SEOs to rank by understanding how Google's systems use topical authority, understand user intent and determine relevancy, despite the fact that these websites are not the helpful and reliable type of site Google wants to rank.

I expect that for many of these sites it's unlikely that Google is eagerly crawling them, looking for new content. But remember, how does Google discover new content? It's by following links on the web. Those links may come from your site (internal links) or from external sources. If Google is not eagerly crawling your site, then you are going to need links from external sources to get your content discovered.

I believe there still are ways to use links and specifically crafted link networks to create enough signals to convince Google's systems to consider your site for ranking. None of the black hats who confidently tell me that they rank via links will share any examples with me. I think their link networks are likely quite valuable to them. And I suspect as Google systems continue to learn, we will see less and less that links that are manufactured to manipulate rankings do anything.

Should you build links?

"Building" is probably the wrong word.

Here are situations where I think there is likely value in working to encourage reputable sites to link to you.

- **If you are truly qualified to talk on your topics, but you are unable to rank on the first page**, then I would recommend working on improving your reputation. Getting links and mentions in places that are already known as trusted sources on your topics is likely to help your site be in the consideration for rankings. There's more to reputation building though than links. Google is using signals from around the web to make these decisions on who is reputable and known for their topics.
- **If you are a local business you can likely improve by becoming more known online**. Links from places that

make sense will help put more information in the world that says, "This business is known for this topic." *However*, we need to remember that there are many other signals that Google can draw from to make their predictions on what a searcher is likely to find helpful. The systems may still use links as a signal, but I expect that Google uses information such as whether people visit your business, whether it is recommended by others, and possibly even whether people tend to buy from you. Should you work on link building as a local business? See the questions below as they will help you decide.

- **If you have a large website such as an E-Commerce site with thousands of products.** If your product pages are struggling, sometimes getting good links to a page can help. It is not easy to get good, natural links (as in not made for SEO reasons) to product pages though. If you want to rank a product page, find ways to get people talking about that product.
- **If you are a new site**. You need Google to find you, so getting mentions and links on the web will help. Keep in mind that Google does not rank websites. Rather, they help people connect with the information they were trying to find on the web. If you have a new business and you are trying to get found online, then you will need to establish a reputation, which includes earning links.

Is this a good link?

Each time I have a discussion about links, I will be asked specific questions about whether or not a link is likely to be good. What about guest post links? Can they be natural? Directories? Are those link signals included in Google's calculations? If I write an article and get it published on an authoritative site, will the link to my site help?

There is a really simple answer to all of these questions.

If the link is one that has value to your business, even if SEO did not matter, then it's good.

Your goal is to produce signals that provide more information that you are a helpful source on your topics. If a link is likely to bring you traffic, truly improve people's opinion or knowledge of your brand, get people talking, and even send you business, then it's a good link.

Where the problem lies is in quantifying its value.

Should you work on building links? Unless you are a brand new site, or are completely unknown and unable to rank for your topics, I would much rather have you spend your time focusing on improving how you can improve on understanding and meeting the needs of your audience.

We talk much more about links in the course. One of my GPTs and Gemini prompts will brainstorm with you on ways to get links and mentions that are likely to improve your reputation on your topics.

Topical Authority, the Knowledge graph, and its topic layer

I hesitated to write this chapter for two reasons. First is because some will take the knowledge in this chapter and use it to do more that resembles manipulation than healthy growth. I think the days where you can use tools and AI to manipulate topical authority are numbered though.

And second, I do not have solid case studies or conclusive evidence to share on *exactly* what needs to be done to improve topical authority. I do believe you can do it in ways that will help improve rankings and *also* will be in line with Google's guidelines. I'll show you some examples of sites that had dramatic improvements after restructuring to improve topical authority. But these sites also made other changes, so we can't say conclusively that the restructuring is what helped.

If you are taking my course I have laid out my full method. My hope is that you will be among the people who try my method and share about it in my community, the Search Bar. It takes a lot of work. You really need to know your topics and thoroughly understand and meet their needs. And you'll need to come up with original, fresh and insightful ideas. We'll get to that soon!

Important: We need to think of people first when we create content. People-first content built with a knowledge of topical authority can be powerful.

I don't think topical authority is as complicated as some make it out to be.

Why I believe we need to pay attention to topical authority

In 2017 I first started recommending something called a hub and spoke architecture in my site audits.

Here is how I described it in a site review I did in early 2017.

> I have recently started recommending something called the Hub and Spoke model to help with content marketing. The idea is that you build a hub that is a main category page. Then, you build satellite pages all around it that are similar in topic. These all link back to the main category page.
>
> For example, you could have a hub called "passive income". On this page you could host your main article on passive income ideas. Then, all other articles that you write that relate to passive income would be the spokes.

This site did extremely well after implementing my advice. I'm not sure what happened to them in 2019 though!

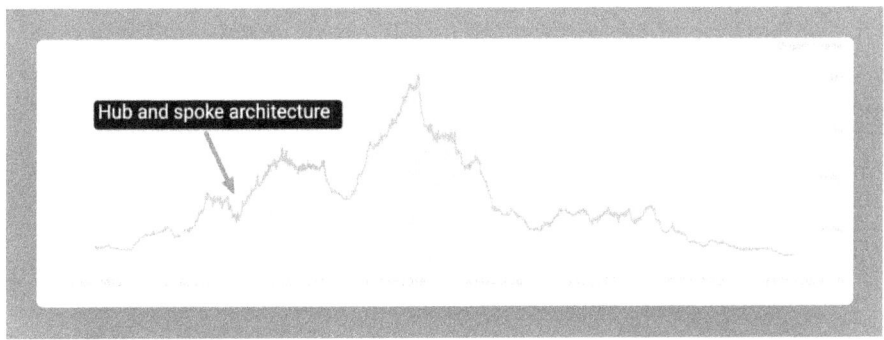

Here is a rudimentary example of a hub and spoke architecture from another site I worked with in 2017. The idea is really simple. If you want to rank for a topic, then write about that topic, and also write a lot of other content that relates to it. Then interlink between pages using anchor text that describes what's important about each page.

This particular site is recognized as a medical authority. They can get away with creating informational content on these topics. For you, your topic spokes should also include pages that provide information that people cannot find elsewhere, but still find valuable when searching on this topic. In reality, the spokes below would also link to each other where it makes sense to do so.

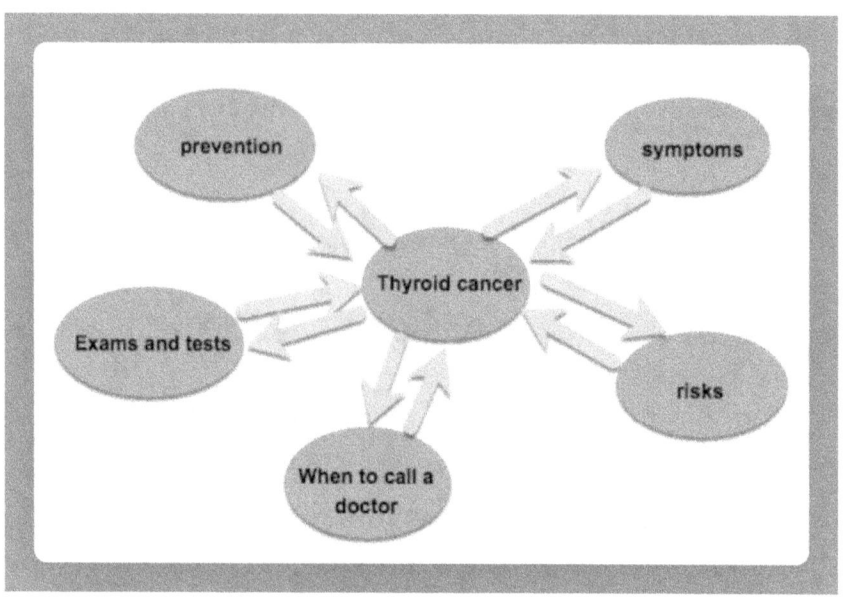

Here is another of the sites that my team and I reviewed in 2017 and brainstormed with, on creating a hub and spoke model. Again this site worked on a lot of things to try and improve site quality. But I really think the content restructuring played a big role in this growth.

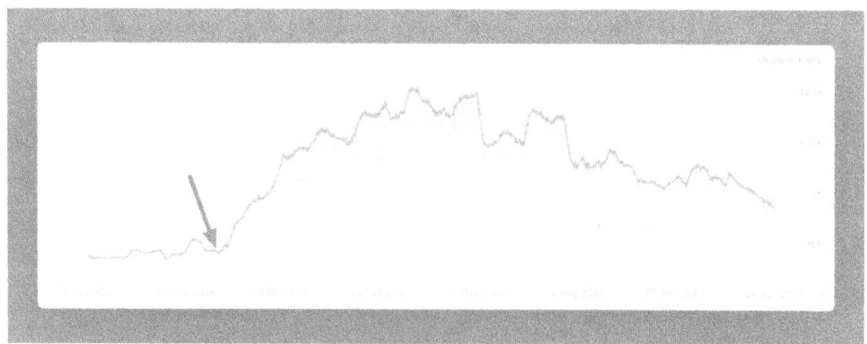

Below is another site that followed this technique. Now, for all of these cases, we can't say conclusively whether the work we did to improve topical authority was what helped, as the reports my team and I delivered often contained over 100 pages of advice and ideas. But this site has done very well.

Until recently. A lot of sites have struggled recently. I believe it's because Google's systems are getting better at recognizing content quality over SEO.

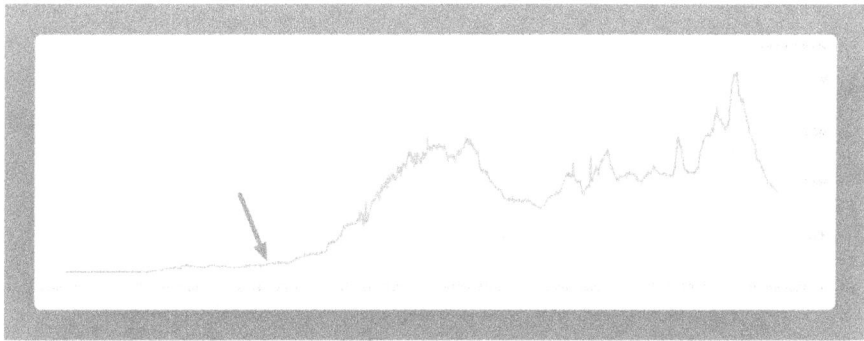

Let's talk more about the blackhats again.

Earlier this year I was contacted by a journalist at Time who was doing an in-depth investigation into a chain of urgent care centers who came out of nowhere to suddenly start ranking for many medical queries, receiving millions of daily visitors to their website.

This site's estimated search traffic skyrocketed until shortly after the Time article was published.

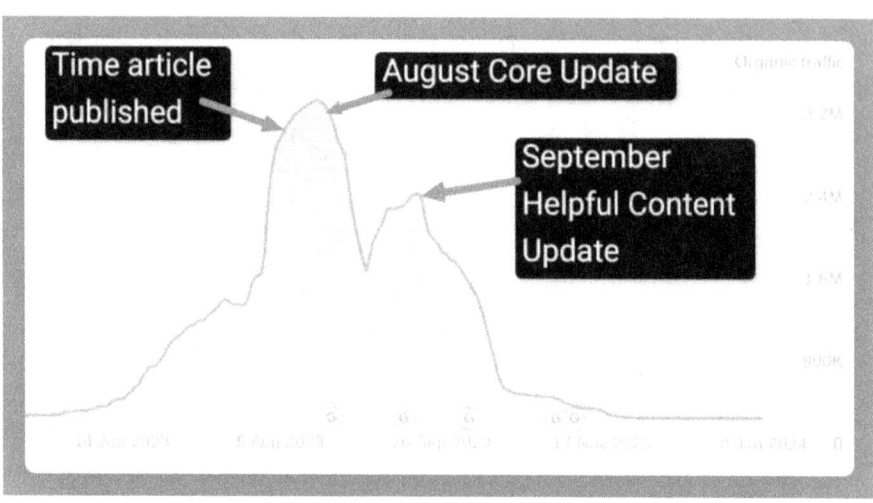

Estimates of organic traffic by Ahrefs.com.

The arrow on the image above is the day the Times' expose[22] was published. We do not know whether the site was manually penalized by Google following this article's publication. I think it's more likely that Google's algorithms dealt with this site's manipulative spam automatically, as there are declines that line up with Google updates. This is what I had predicted would happen:

> Haynes, the SEO consultant, says this type of SEO tactic is unlikely to work for long. For one thing, Google is currently implementing an AI content system that is built to detect "unhelpful" content, and, according to Haynes, many of Nao's nonsense posts would likely fall into this category. So Google will catch up with Nao sooner or later.

---

[22] This Urgent Care Clinic Is Flooding the Internet With Nonsensical Posts. Is AI to Blame? Alana Semuels. Time. 9 August, 2023.
https://time.com/6302710/nao-medical-google-ai/

The question that I was asked by the reporter was *why* they were creating copious amounts of AI generated content. How did it benefit them?

> You might go to an urgent care facility's website to make an appointment or read an explanation of what causes fevers. But most people are probably not looking to urgent care websites for an explanation of what happens when unicorns consume ketamine.
>
> But that—and millions of other pages about things that don't make much sense—have suddenly been popping up on the website of a New York City-based urgent care clinic called Nao Medical. The company, which says it has 16 locations in New York City and Long Island, appears to be using AI to generate a vast flood of well-written and sensibly structured—but not particularly accurate—posts about popular topics in an effort to rank higher on Google.

From Time: This Urgent Care Clinic Is Flooding the Internet With Nonsensical Posts. Is AI to Blame?

My research found that the site was ranking well for a lot of phrases such as "caffeine and autism". A search for "site:[thissite.com] caffeine and autism" showed me 22 different pages that talked about this same topic:

- Caffeine and Autism: What You Need to Know
- Understanding the Connection Between Caffeine and Autism
- Autism and Caffeine: Understanding the Connection

...and so on.

The articles were, to me, clearly AI written, with each covering the topic from a slightly different angle. Most really weren't *bad* content. They covered the topic well and answered all of the questions that a searcher would have.

It's important for me to note here that my intention is not to encourage you to spam Google with different articles that cover every aspect of your topic. Nor is it to use AI to completely write your articles for you. It is so tempting to slide down the path of focusing on what Google rewards all the while trying to convince ourselves that we're doing what's best for our audience. **We need to think of our users first**. If you can truly focus on your users and do this alongside a knowledge of topical authority, this is your best chance to see great success.

There were multiple tactics that this site appeared to be using to manipulate Google rankings. It worked well until Google's helpful content system eventually figured out that these pages were not the ideal ones to show searchers. If you want to create a website that lasts, it is not a good idea to flirt with producing content that does not comply with Google's guidelines[23] and also Google's advice on using AI generated content[24].

---

[23] Spam policies for Google web search. Google.
https://developers.google.com/search/docs/essentials/spam-policies
[24] Google Search's Guidance about AI-generated content/ Google.
https://developers.google.com/search/blog/2023/02/google-search-and-ai-content

What I want to focus on most in studying this site, of all of their blackhat tactics, is the wild amount of content this site was creating. They had so many articles. Some made sense and were potentially helpful. Some were bizarre.

> One post on Nao Medical's website explains a medical condition it calls "Derek Jeter Herpes Tree," which is not actually a medical condition but that Nao says nevertheless is "a rare viral infection" that affects trees. There are posts promising that Ivermectin can help COVID-19 patients regain their sense of smell (not true), about getting iodine poisoning from eating too much shrimp (extremely unlikely), about a "cutting-edge technology" called the Cloud 5 Zinc Shell (not a real thing) and a "revolutionary healthcare solution" called Chicken Par Y (not a real thing either.) Google just about anything you can think of and "Nao Medical" and you will find a long list of posts, some of which appear to make some sense, others which don't.

This site's strategy appeared to be to create topical hubs of a small number of pages of content that is connected to one topic.

I expect they figured out that topics are important to Google's systems.

Google's knowledge graph has an entire layer that is dedicated to topics.

Let's talk about the knowledge graph and then I'm going to attempt to get you all excited about the topic layer.

The knowledge graph

You've likely heard of Google's knowledge graph. In Google's documentation called, How Google's Knowledge Graph works[25], published in 2012, they tell us it is a collection of billions of facts. Picture that...a giant cloud of facts, all interconnected to each other.

The intelligence in the knowledge graph is not in its ability to hold facts, but rather, to understand the *connections* between those facts.

Remember Larry Page's dream about downloading all of the links on the web?

When you search for Sundar Pichai, it's the knowledge graph that contains the information that tells us what's important to know on this topic. Connected to the topic of the entity "Sundar Pichai" are the topics, "CEO of Google", his age, and his education.

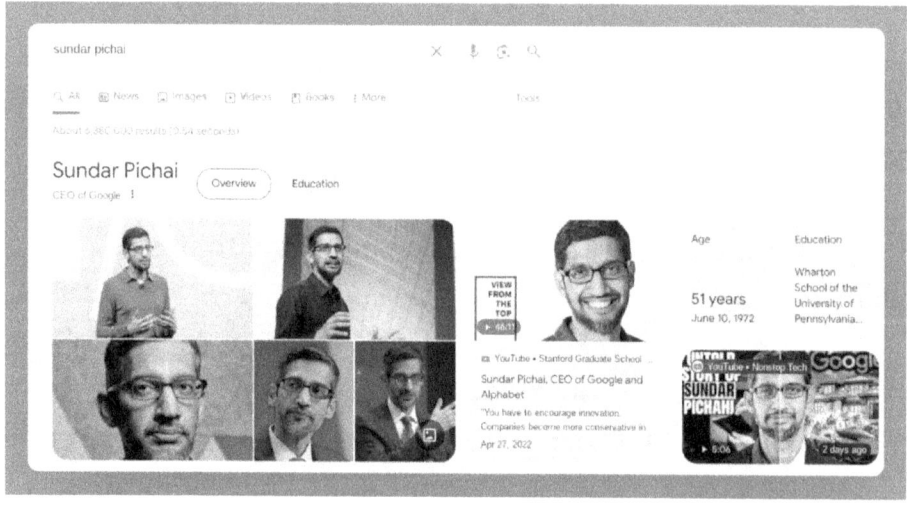

---

[25] How Google's Knowledge Graph works. Google. Retrieved Jan 2024. https://support.google.com/knowledgepanel/answer/9787176?hl=en

The knowledge graph was launched in May of 2012, just a few weeks following the first release of the infamous Penguin algorithmic filter which decimated many sites that previously had benefited from low quality link building. Are the two connected? You bet they are.

As Google learns to rely on AI systems to identify which content is likely to be helpful and reliable, many of the signals they relied on previously become less important. It's not like links suddenly stopped working. Rather, Google continually gets better at learning which signals to use in their calculations and then machine learning systems determine how much weight to give those signals. **Links have gradually moved from being the most important signal to help Google understand the world, to one of many signals** that can be used.

The knowledge graph is a key component of Google's ability to understand the world.

Google knows that when you search for a particular entity (a person, a thing, a topic), you likely are interested in certain related topics that are connected to that entity.

Their recent $60 million Reddit deal gives them even more insight into the questions that people tend to ask on any topic. Google told us in 2012 that they've been **working on an intelligent model, a graph that understands real world entities and their relationships to one another.**

> Take a query like [taj mahal]. For more than four decades, search has essentially been about matching keywords to queries. To a search engine the words [taj mahal] have been just that—two words.
>
> But we all know that [taj mahal] has a much richer meaning. You might think of one of the world's most beautiful monuments, or a Grammy Award-winning musician, or possibly even a casino in Atlantic City, NJ. Or, depending on when you last ate, the nearest Indian restaurant. It's why we've been working on an intelligent model—in geek-speak, a "graph"—that understands real-world entities and their relationships to one another: things, not strings.

From Google's introduction to the knowledge graph in 2012[26]

Google goes on in that blog post to tell us that the knowledge graph is the first step in the **next generation of search.**

We'll get back to topical authority in a moment. Let's first talk about this next generation of search that Google started building with the knowledge graph because it helps us understand how Google understands topics.

The next generation of search

This next generation of search taps into the "collective intelligence of the web and understands the world a bit more like people do."

> The Knowledge Graph enables you to search for things, people or places that Google knows about—landmarks, celebrities, cities, sports teams, buildings, geographical features, movies, celestial objects, works of art and more—and instantly get information that's relevant to your query. This is a critical first step towards building the next generation of search, which taps into the collective intelligence of the web and understands the world a bit more like people do.

---

[26] Introducing the Knowledge Graph: things, not strings. Google. May 16, 2012. https://blog.google/products/search/introducing-knowledge-graph-things-not/

In the year 2000, Google's Co-Founder, Larry Page told us[27] that several people at Google were working on building an artificial intelligence that could give you the perfect answer based on the information on the web.

"We have some people at Google who are really trying to build artificial intelligence and to do it on a large scale and so on. And in fact, to make search better, we really need to make, you know, **to do a perfect job of search you could ask any query and it would give you the perfect answer and that would be artificial intelligence, right? Based on everything being on the web, which is a pretty close approximation.**"

He said that Google has been moving incrementally closer to this.

I believe that every Google update we have seen represents Google moving *slightly* closer to being able to use the intelligence that exists on the web to give a perfect answer to every query.

Every time Google gave us a metric to shoot for, whether it was https, core web vital scores or even giving us

---

[27] Larry Page Compares Artificial Intelligence to Human DNA. YouTube. Recorded 2000. Posted 2011.
https://www.youtube.com/watch?v=unk8RpIrNuM&t=2s

opportunities to rank in rich features like FAQs in the search results, we worked collectively alongside Google, helping the web improve and become more helpful and reliable, and better understood by machines.

We have been working incrementally closer to helping Google create a perfect AI system that can answer any question.

Google told us in their announcement of their AI chatbot, Bard[28], now renamed to Gemini, that Bard "seeks to combine **the breadth of the world's knowledge with the power, intelligence and creativity of [their] large language models.**"

The knowledge graph, Google's understanding of the world and the connections between the entities within it, is very important to Google's AI.

As I write this, we are awaiting the launch of the Gemini App (formerly Assistant with Bard)[29] which will bring Google's large language model AI chatbot Gemini to anyone with an iPhone or Android. Google says the AI conversational overlay will change how we interact with our phones. Gemini is not a search engine. It's an AI assistant. Eventually it will be one that can take actions on our behalf.

---

[28] An important next step on our AI journey. Sundar Pichai. Google. February 6, 2023. https://blog.google/technology/ai/bard-google-ai-search-updates/

[29] Assistant with Bard: A step toward a more personal assistant. Google. October 24, 2023. https://blog.google/products/assistant/google-assistant-bard-generative-ai/

With each Gemini update it improves[30].

> **2023.09.27**
>
> **Help Bard improve side by side**
> - **What:** We've added a new way for you to give feedback. When Bard occasionally responds with 2 drafts side by side, select the draft you prefer. You can also indicate no preference or opt out entirely.
> - **Why: Real-world feedback helps Bard improve the quality of its responses.** Your feedback on Bard drafts contributes to making Bard better for yourself and others.

It is trained on the web and, if you use the Double-Check with Google button, it verifies its output across information from the web. Gemini will be an easy way for anyone to ask any question and receive an answer that is derived from Google's understanding of the world and the important connections related to the topic you have searched.

It is very important that the search results that Google recommends are reliable. We are almost there. I do not believe that Google would launch Gemini in Google Assistant, and more recently AI overviews in Search, unless they felt it could consistently give reliable, helpful answers to any question asked.

Some have argued that no one will use Assistant. I think Google will gradually make changes so that more and more of us are getting their answers from AI and finding it helpful. While it is not perfect and you can easily find faults that Google is working to correct, it is so helpful!

---

[30] Bard Updates. Google. Retrieved Jan 2024. https://bard.google.com/updates

Google's Search Liaison Danny Sullivan has told us a few times near the end of 2023 that significant changes to search are on the way. Perhaps as you read this we are navigating through the period of time in which Danny has advised us to "buckle up," as significant changes are about to take place in search[31].

Danny's exact words were:

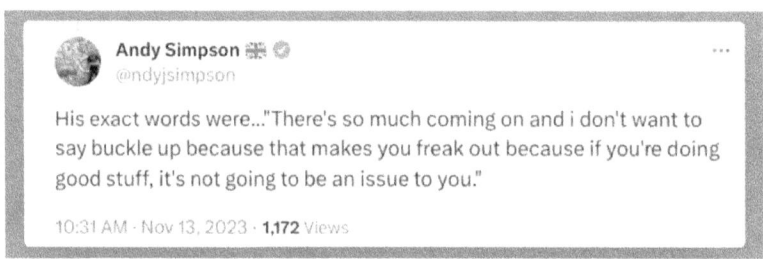

Andy Simpson on X[32]

"If you're doing good stuff, it's not going to be an issue to you."

I believe we will see a number of updates that are equally, if not more catastrophic to some businesses as recent core and helpful content updates have been. The businesses most affected will be those whose success in ranking comes from

---

[31] Google says major changes coming to search rankings. Barry Schwartz. Search Engine Land. November 13, 2023.
https://searchengineland.com/google-says-major-changes-coming-to-search-rankings-434548

[32] Tweet from Andy Simpson who was at the Brighton SEO conference, quoting Danny Sullivan. Nov 13, 2023.
https://x.com/ndyjsimpson/status/1724087513860476964?s=20

understanding Google more than understanding what's helpful to their audience.

The March core update of 2024 represented the start of these significant changes.

Gemini

Google recently changed the language model that powers Bard. This is the model that Bard uses to understand the world, the topics within it, and how they are all interconnected. The advancement that allowed for this is a new model called Gemini. Gemini not only understands the connections between *words* on the internet, but also can understand *images and video*. I expect that Gemini gave Google a dramatic improvement in its ability to understand the world and its connections.

It wasn't just the Bard chatbot that was dramatically improved by Gemini. This technology likely also improved search as Gemini is Google's foundation model. It underpins their AI capabilities across their products.

It would not surprise me if the reason why Danny Sullivan has told us to "buckle up" is because **Gemini has given Google an even stronger understanding of the world, and the connections between the topics it contains.**

In February of 2024, Gemini was updated with a brand new infrastructure that uses something called a Mixture of

Experts model to make it even faster and better. AI is going to continue to learn and improve very quickly.

Google has been telling us for years that they build algorithms to assess site quality. The first time we saw what I now call the helpful content guidance[33], was in Google's documentation that accompanied the rollout of the Panda algorithmic filter in 2011[34].

> **What counts as a high-quality site?**
>
> Our site quality algorithms are aimed at helping people find "high-quality" sites by reducing the rankings of low-quality content. The recent "Panda" change tackles the difficult task of algorithmically assessing website quality. Taking a step back, we wanted to explain some of the ideas and research that drive the development of our algorithms.
>
> Below are some questions that one could use to assess the "quality" of a page or an article. These are the kinds of questions we ask ourselves as we write algorithms that attempt to assess site quality. Think of it as our take at encoding what we think our users want.
>
> Of course, we aren't disclosing the actual ranking signals used in our algorithms because we don't want folks to game our search results, but if you want to step into Google's mindset, the questions below provide some guidance on how we've been looking at the issue:
>
> - Would you trust the information presented in this article?
> - Is this article written by an expert or enthusiast who knows the topic well, or is it more shallow in nature?
> - Does the site have duplicate, overlapping, or redundant articles on the same or similar topics with slightly different keyword variations?
> - Would you be comfortable giving your credit card information to this site?
> - Does this article have spelling, stylistic, or factual errors?
> - Are the topics driven by genuine interests of readers of the site, or does the site generate content by attempting to guess what might rank well in search engines?
> - Does the article provide original content or information, original reporting, original research, or original analysis?

---

[33] Creating helpful, reliable, people-first content. Google.
https://developers.google.com/search/docs/fundamentals/creating-helpful-content

[34] More guidance on building high-quality sites. Google.
https://developers.google.com/search/blog/2011/05/more-guidance-on-building-high-quality

These algorithms have been evolving for years. With each one Google gets incrementally closer to the web they want to present. Gemini is the next step in technology that improves search so that it is most likely to return results that are consistently reliable and helpful.

If you're truly a business or personality that people seek out as a source of information on your topics, and if you're creating content that people are finding helpful, then you are much more likely to already be aligning with Google's Helpful Content Guidance than an SEO who is attempting to manipulate topical authority. As the system continues to improve, legitimacy will be a strength. Being authentic and known for being helpful will be super powers.

If you can do both - create truly helpful content and do it in a way that creates a body of helpful content on your topic, this is the key to creating topical authority.

If you're somewhere in the middle and not sure whether you're creating content for an audience that seeks you out or perhaps you're creating content for search engines, hopefully the rest of this book will help you decide whether you truly can create the type of people-first content that Google has been building their systems to reward.

In the course we go much deeper into exploring the topic layer. I share in great detail my method and some exercises to help you determine what topics to choose, what subtopics to focus on, whether you should consider restructuring your urls, and what words to use as anchor text in your links between this hub and spoke content.

Structured data

I have a confession to make. I really don't like talking about schema. Throughout my career there are two things that I have dreaded discussing with website owners - schema and hreflang. I still don't feel I know enough about either and have great respect for those of you who have these topics mastered.

For at least 10 years now I have promised myself that one day I would dig in more to understand schema and its potential value. Recently I did it. I dedicated one full day to learning and writing everything I can about schema. And wow, after writing this, I am definitely seeing more value in adding schema, especially as we see more AI used in finding information.

First, I am embarrassed to admit that I didn't understand when I should use the term schema and when I should use structured data. I'm going to say it because if I'm confused I'm betting there are others out there who are as well.

I asked my Google Assistant (not yet Gemini, which I expect it will be by the time this book comes out) what the difference is.

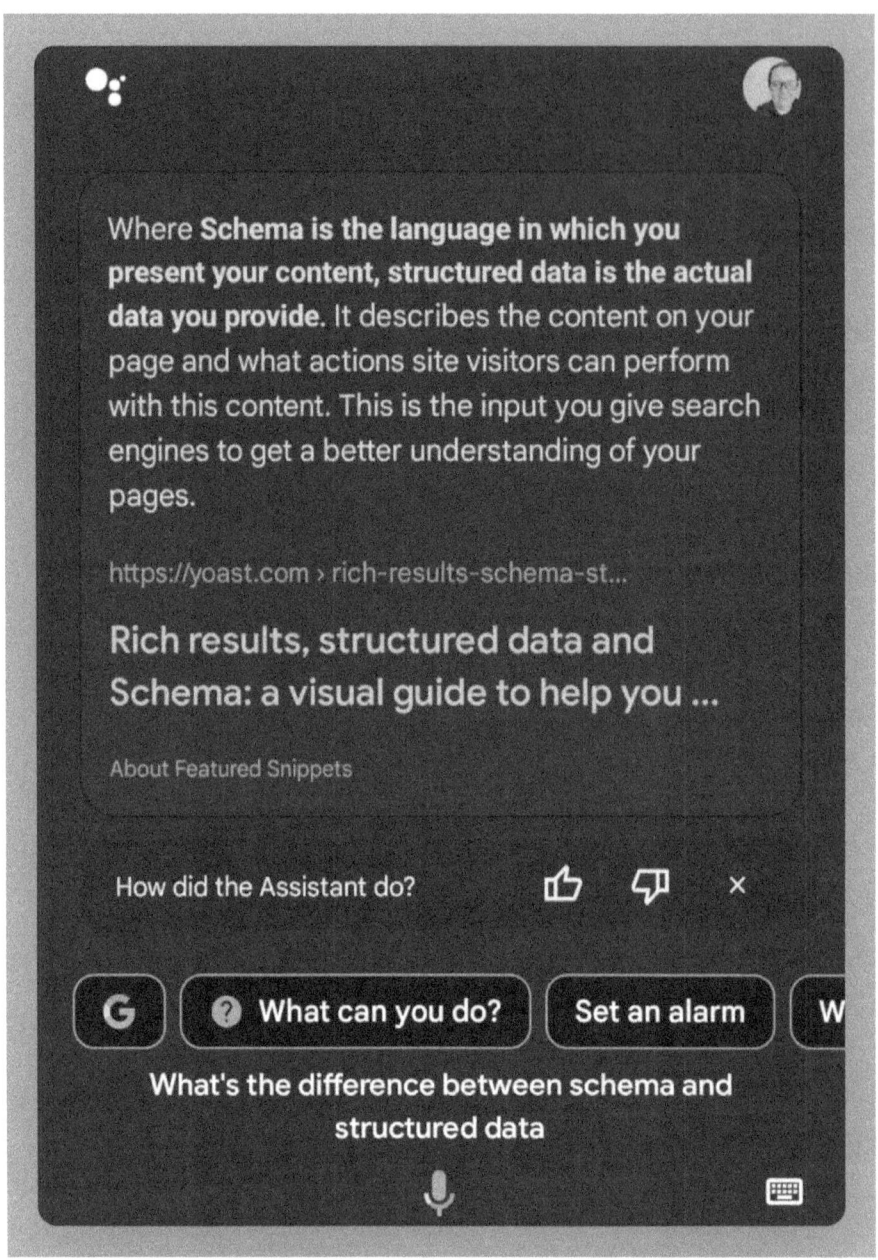

Schema is like a language that search engines understand. It's a way for websites to describe their content to search engines, like an instruction manual that helps search engines understand your business and its offerings.

100

You can communicate this information using different formats - JSON-LD, Microdata that is embedded in HTML or RDFa (flexible tags.) There are lots of resources you can find to help you learn how to implement structured data, including Google's guidance.

> Google Search works hard to understand the content of a page. You can help us by providing explicit clues about the meaning of a page to Google by including structured data on the page. Structured data is a standardized format for providing information about a page and classifying the page content; for example, on a recipe page, what are the ingredients, the cooking time and temperature, the calories, and so on.

It sounds like understanding a page better with the help of structured data is important to Google, but they give us little solid reason as to why it is important *to us*, other than for the types of schema that we can implement that can give us rich results in the search results.

> # Structured data markup that Google Search supports Send feedback
>
> Google uses structured data to understand the content on the page and show that content in a richer appearance in search results, which is called a *rich result*. To make your site eligible for appearance as one of these rich results, follow the guide to learn how to implement structured data on your site. If you're just getting started, visit Understand how structured data works.

While schema is the *language* that allows us to communicate more about our pages to search engines, **structured data** is the *information* that is being communicated such as the name of an author or the topic of an article. It's structured in a way that is easy for computers to understand.

Structured data is the language machines understand. It's the information that Google's systems can use. Schema is like the interface that allows us to communicate with machines that use that language. Google's goal is to be able to understand all data, not just structured data. Understanding the structured data is part of the process.

By the way, if you're looking for a good movie to watch this weekend, Arrival would be a perfect one. It's a story of learning to communicate with an alien species. It really moved me.

When we add schema to label the structured data on our websites, we are making things as clear as possible for Google. But, Google says it does not give us any sort of ranking boost.

Until recently, I have not understood what the benefit to **me** is to spend hours learning about schema and then deciding how to implement it. I suppose my next decision will be deciding whether I use a tool like InLinks or Schema App, or perhaps a WordPress plugin. Or perhaps there is a better solution. Going down the road of implementing schema is not a light and easy task.

But I think for some of you, it could be something that is worthwhile.

Is schema a ranking factor?

We likely should move away from using the words "ranking factor". As more and more AI systems determine what is shown to people, the idea of singular ranking factors makes less sense. What we really want to know is whether there is going to be a benefit to us if we take the time to implement schema markup. And if so, which schema should we focus on? There is no end to the connections you can help Google make in regards to your content.

But why do it?

Some types of schema can give you a special appearance in the search results. Those can alter consumer behaviour. You can add schema to show review stars. Or schema to show the pros and cons of a product perhaps. Recently Google added a new type of schema you can add that highlights forum discussions and even individuals posting in forums in some search results.

What I am most interested in learning more about is **whether there is benefit to your organic search performance that comes from adding the types of schema that don't give you rich results**.

Let's look at this case study published by Dixon Jones of InLinks, a tool that helps you with all of this. I have not personally used InLinks, but I know several people who do and find it quite helpful. Also, Dixon and I have had some really good conversations on this type of thing. He is one smart cookie!

[Case Study: Does Webpage Schema (About & Mentions) Improve Rankings?](#)

20 different SEOs participated in this experiment where they tested adding About and Mentions schema markup.

Before we talk about the results of the study, let's first talk about what About and Mentions schema are.

[About schema](#) is language that tells Google, or machines that understand schema, what the **topic of your page is**.

[Mentions schema]() is language that tells machines which **related topics** you are covering as well.

Can you see why I am interested in this? If you have not yet read the section of this book that discusses the [topic layer](), it may be worth doing that before moving on in this section.

We have been talking a lot lately about the importance of being known for your topics, and also, of having a wealth of helpful content on the topics that are likely to be important to your audience.

As I've been saying throughout this book, the more I study Google papers and documentation, here's what I think is most important when it comes to being recommended by Google today, and even more so as AI changes how people interact with search:

- **Be known as a helpful resource for people who want to learn about the topic you write about.**
- **Create a wealth of information on that topic, and those that are related to it, that your audience is likely to find helpful.**

If being *known for your topics* is important to Google, and if *schema can help us explain to Google what topics and subtopics we are covering*, it only stands to reason that we should be paying attention to schema!

We want to do all we can to help Google understand the topics and subtopics we have content on.

Let's look at some examples of schema in use. Let's say I have an article that is about a new iPhone that was just announced and the topic of this page is the most recent Apple announcement. Schema.org says I can use About schema to tell search engines:

- this page is about an event
- the name of the event is this

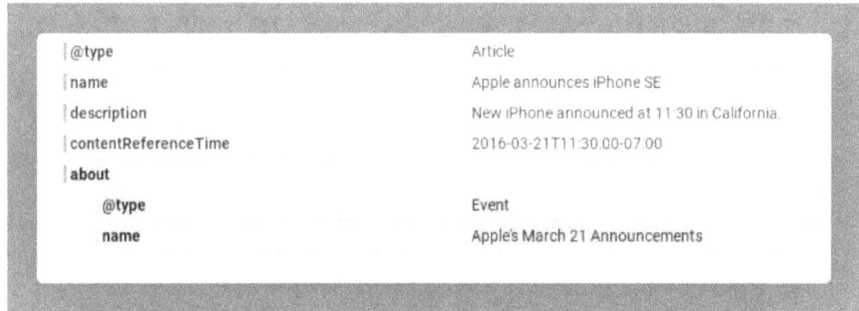

Let's say you had a blog post on the topic of artificial intelligence. You could use About schema that links that blog post to the Wikipedia page on AI to help search engines understand that that's the same topic you are talking on.

Bard gave me this next example. Notice how not only did Bard use About schema, it chose to also show me Mentions schema. This article's *main* topic is AI. It *also mentions* machine learning and natural language processing.

106

```
Here are some examples of how About schema is properly used:

1. Blog Post About a Specific Topic:

HTML

<script type="application/ld+json">
{
  "@context": "https://schema.org",
  "@type": "WebPage",
  "about": "https://en.wikipedia.org/wiki/Artificial_intelligence",
  "mentions": [
    "https://en.wikipedia.org/wiki/Machine_learning",
    "https://en.wikipedia.org/wiki/Natural_language_processing"
  ]
}
</script>

Use code with caution. Learn more
```

The topic layer of the knowledge graph (again)

OK, let's revisit this topic layer of the knowledge graph. I asked Bard to help me conceptualize the topic layer.

Bard told me to think of the knowledge graph as a vast landscape where entities are the landmarks and the relationships between them are like paths. The topic layer, then, is another layer atop this landscape, like a network of invisible air currents that shape the flow of meaning across the terrain.

I thought that was beautiful. I used Chat to make an image to represent this (above). Then asked for its "thoughts".

> **ChatGPT**
>
> The analogy you described for understanding a knowledge graph is quite illustrative and helpful in visualizing complex digital structures in a more tangible way. In a knowledge graph, entities (like people, places, things, concepts, etc.) are indeed analogous to landmarks in a vast landscape. These entities are interconnected through various types of relationships, much like the paths or roads that connect landmarks in a physical landscape.
>
> The "topic layer" in this analogy, described as a network of invisible air currents, can be seen as a representation of the overarching themes, contexts, or categories that influence or define the relationships and meanings among these entities. This layer adds an additional dimension to the understanding of a knowledge graph, emphasizing how broader concepts or themes can impact the flow and interconnection of information.
>
> While no analogy is perfect, this one effectively conveys the complex and interconnected nature of knowledge graphs. It emphasizes both the individual entities and their relationships, as well as the higher-level influences that guide and shape these connections. This visualization can be particularly useful for conceptualizing how information is structured and interconnected in a way that's not immediately visible but is nonetheless influential in determining how knowledge is organized and accessed.

Let's look at another example.

If you had a product page for a coffee maker, Bard says you could tell Google about the topic, coffee maker, using About schema. And also you could use Mentions schema to tell search engines this product is related to the topics coffee and brewing.

```
2. Product Page for a Specific Item:

HTML

<script type="application/ld+json">
{
  "@context": "https://schema.org",
  "@type": "WebPage",
  "about": "https://en.wikipedia.org/wiki/Coffee_maker",
  "mentions": [
    "https://en.wikipedia.org/wiki/Coffee",
    "https://en.wikipedia.org/wiki/Brewing"
  ]
}
</script>
```

You can go even further in telling search engines what your content is about by adding SameAs schema.

Here is an example from Schema.org that shows the author of the book Hitchhiker's Guide to the Galaxy (My all time favourite book. As if his reference number in his schema is 42,) is the same author that is listed on a particular wikidata page.

This is why I've recommended in the past that if you are trying to get known for your topics, it can help to use SameAs schema to help Google understand exactly who the author is.

109

You're helping Google connect the dots to better understand who you are.

What I hadn't considered before is using **SameAs to tell Google which topic is the same.** Here is an example given from inLinks. In this example, they have helped search engines understand that:

- this page is about search engine optimization
- this topic is the same as the one that is discussed on the Wikipedia page for search engine optimization.

or, in another example, for topics that could have multiple meanings:

- the topic of this page is trapping.
- this is the type of trapping that is the same as what is discussed on this particular Wikipedia page.

```
"about": [
    {"@type": "Thing", "name": "Search_engine_optimization", "sameAs": "https://en.wikipedia.org/wiki/Search_engine_optimization"},
    {"@type": "Thing", "name": "WordPress", "sameAs": "https://en.wikipedia.org/wiki/WordPress"},
    {"@type": "Thing", "name": "trap", "sameAs": "https://en.wikipedia.org/wiki/Trapping"}
],
```

The InLinks study recruited a bunch of SEOs to test putting About and Mentions schema on some pages, but not others. They found that **over a month, twice as many pages with schema gained rankings compared to those that lost rankings.**

It's a small study, but worth considering.

Dixon told me that yes, there can be ranking benefit from adding schema to help machines better understand your content. But sometimes the opposite can happen! Google may start ranking you for less as it gets better at understanding what your focus is. The good news is that if that happens, those queries you were previously ranking for probably weren't relevant to user intent anyway.

Now that I understand more about schema I am getting excited about it.

The experiences of the SEO community

I asked the SEO's on X to share their experiences with using Schema. Did it help improve rankings?

Jarno van Driel, shared this presentation from 2015 in which he used structured data to help a medical practice develop their knowledge graph and recover following big losses with an early Panda update. They added markup for **physician, MedicalClinic** and **Person (surgeon).** They used sameAs schema to link to social profiles and more to help connect the dots.

They then began to have much more of their important information about the business show up in the search results and in their knowledge panel. But, there were no changes in organic traffic that resulted.

The hypothesis they developed was that the site's large number of pages, with many targeting overlapping keywords, was making it hard for Google to understand what was important to each topic.

This is as Jarno pointed out, part of Google's Panda guidance:

> The moment when *Amit Singhal*
> finally started to make sense
>
> - Does the site have duplicate, overlapping, or redundant articles on the same or similar topics with slightly different keyword variations?

So, they ran a test and added schema to make it more clear which topics were covered in each article, but months later not much had changed in terms of rankings.

Next, they added Article schema. Apologies as the original image is blurry. The main point of this diagram I'd like to emphasize is that this is essentially a mini knowledge graph for this page that explains the topics within it, and does much more to help machines understand the connections.

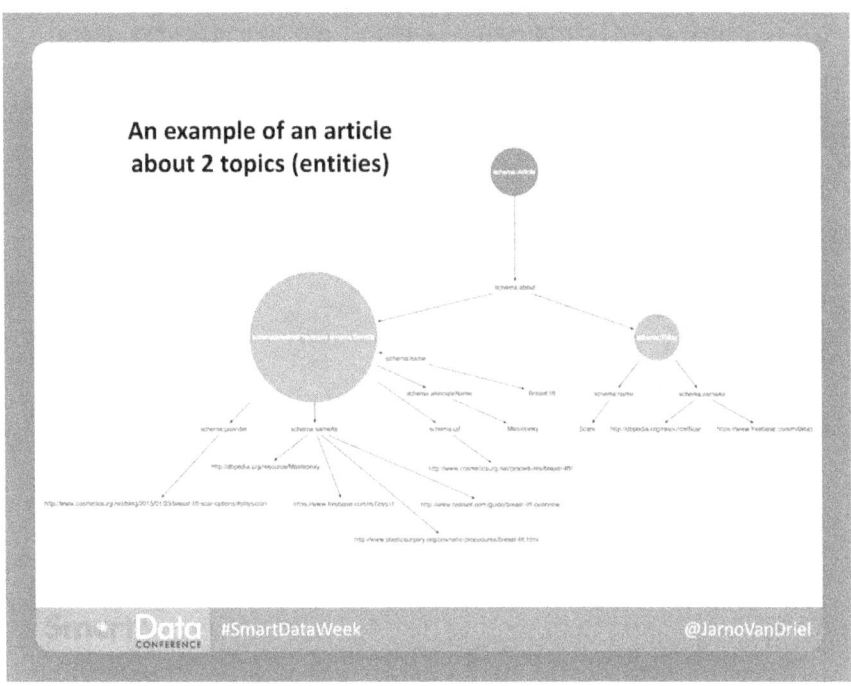

This article is about two entities:

- a medical procedure / service (breast lift surgery)
- a thing (scars)

This medical procedure / service:

- is named breast lift
- is the same as mastopexy
- is the same as the procedure described on the plasticsurgery.org page for breast lift

Scars are the same as the freebase page on the topic of scars.

Essentially, they made it more clear what the main topics of each page were, and helped Google understand more about exactly what those topics are.

This seems to have helped!

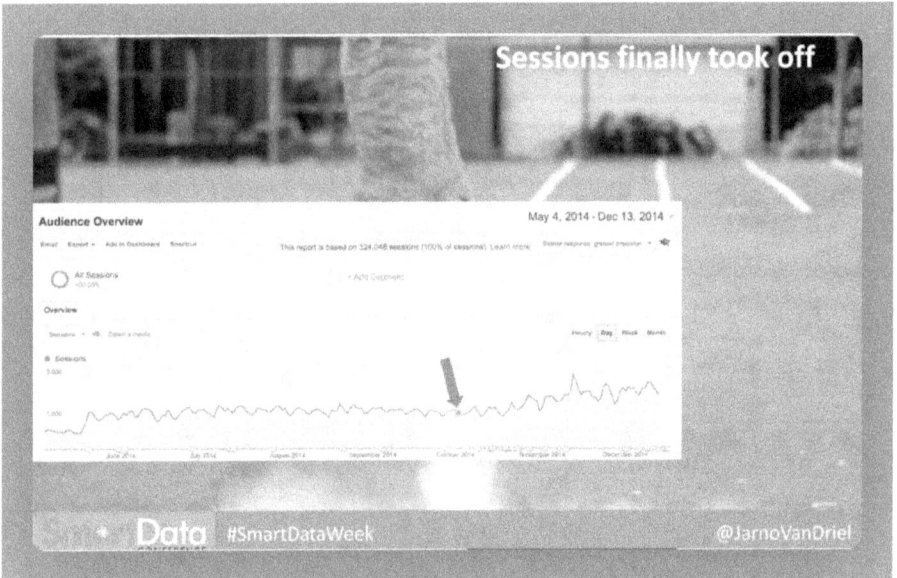

The presentation goes on to discuss how you can test the impact of adding schema. It is worth spending time reading it.

If you're still with me, which is surprising considering I've asked you to spend ages reading about the topic of schema, so far we have seen that just adding schema is likely to have significant benefit. But two studies now have shown that there does appear to be *some* benefit that could be gained in regards to organic performance by adding markup to help search engines better understand your topics.

What about AI? Where does structured data fit in?

I have speculated about how Google's ranking systems have gradually added more and more dependence on AI to their systems. Get ready. We are about to get technical again.

Throughout [Pandu Nayak's testimony in the DOJ vs Google antitrust trial](), they discuss the use of systems that work by doing something called embedding.

You have heard me talk about vector embeddings. They are very important to language models like GPT. In the next chapter on intent, we are going to talk much more about vectors.

Embeddings are also important to Google.

Let's look at what Nayak tells us about one of Google's important systems, RankEmbed. It is one of the systems that is involved in retrieval of search results.

> A. Some of the deep learning systems are also involved in the retrieval process, like we discussed, like the RankEmbed system.
>
> Q. Yes, but --
>
> A. But unless we retrieve the right documents, you can't score them, yes.
>
> Q. But most of the retrieval process happens under the core system, right?
>
> A. Other than, as I said, the RankEmbed thing also does retrieval.
>
> **THE COURT:** I'm sorry, you said RankEmbed?
>
> **THE WITNESS:** Yes. RankEmbed bought one of those deep learning systems that also does retrieval.

They often refer to RankEmbed as RankEmbed BERT. Just as ChatGPT uses the language model called GPT, when it comes to search, Google uses this model, RankEmbed BERT - a version of BERT trained specifically for use in ranking.

This model is trained on click data from real users and fine-tuned with the information gained from quality raters on which pages are likely helpful or not and what characteristics of the page helped form that decision.

> Q. And I'm not going to say the percentage, because I think that those are off limits, but RankEmbed BERT is trained on click and query data, right?
> A. Yes, it is.
> Q. And then it's fine-tuned on human IS rater data?
> A. Yes, it is.

RankEmbed can help Google find new pages to add to the results that are possibly helpful that weren't identified by traditional retrieval.

> Q. RankEmbed identifies a few more documents to add those identified by the traditional retrieval?
> A. That is correct, for some definition of few.

Let's talk about vector spaces. The GPT language model (what's in ChatGPT) operates within a vector space that understands the *relationships between words*. Gemini 1.5's LLMs operate in a vector space that also understands the *relationships between not only words, but also* **images and videos** as well.

I picture RankEmbed as a vector space that understands the relationships between the structured data that can be extracted from a webpage.

If we provide Google with schema, we are helping them extract the structured data. We're helping them understand the important information on our pages. Eventually though, it's Google's goal to be able to extract the important bits without us having to label it all.

This is just a theory for now, but here's what Chat thought of my idea. I promise it's worth spending some energy trying to digest this response.

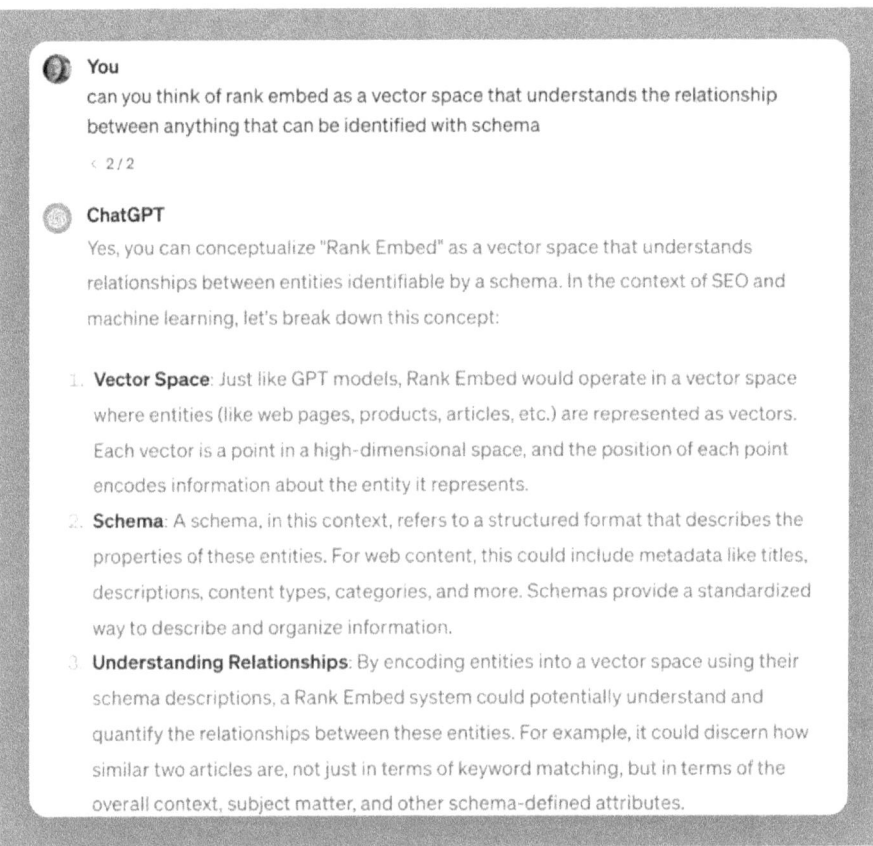

I had a realization about vector embeddings at Pubcon a few months ago. At this conference I asked Google's Gary Illyes whether it was worthwhile learning more about vector embeddings. He paused and said, yes. But only because it is interesting. He said it would not give us an advantage in

Search. The question must have impacted him because he brought it up a couple of times during his keynote speech.

After talking to Gary I could not stop thinking about vector embeddings.

I dreamed about them.

I watched the Matrix.

I even started to read [Einstein's theory of relativity](#).

I can't stop thinking about how our picture of the world that we live in is created from our understanding of the relationships between the information in whatever vector space it is that we are in.

At Google I/O, Jeff Dean said, AI is about how "different things inform each other."

Even though Gary said it wouldn't help, I put together a theory to use my new knowledge of vector embeddings to see if I could improve content and make it even more likely to be seen as the most helpful and relevant result simply by crafting the text in a way that better understood and met user intent.

I mean, it makes sense, right? Google can understand the query. And they use AI to match it with content that is likely to meet the searcher's intent. The words used on a page are incredibly important.

Early tests of this method are quite promising.

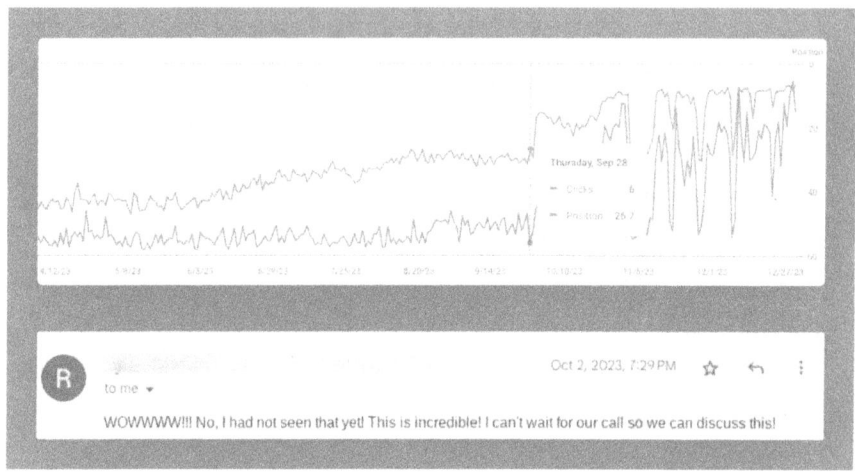

Intent (and oh boy let's talk vector embeddings, fine-tuning and more)

Of all of the chapters I have written in this book, this is the one that is the most important. We're going to theorize on how Google understands user intent. If we can understand our queries like Google does, then we can produce content that is even more likely to be seen as helpful to both users and search engines.

Combine this knowledge with content that is borne from the true needs of your audience, and you suddenly have content that is even more helpful because it understands the intent of the searcher and does well to meet it.

We're going to dig deeper into understanding a fascinating topic - vector embeddings. There is a lot of theory in this section. And more in the course if you want to dig deeper.

Don't worry if some of this information is complicated. At the end, I'll summarize it all into the bits we can consider as we improve our content.

Vector embeddings are a way of converting words, images and other data into numerical values. The process involves mapping these data points into a large, multi-dimensional space. In this space, similar items end up being placed closer to each other, forming patterns based on their similarities. Each item in this space is represented by a unique series of numbers. Here's a super simple example:

- "cat": (0.65, 0.3, -0.2)
- "pet": (0.8, 0.15, -0.1)

This numerical array captures the relationships between this item and others in the vector space that are close in similarity. Each number in the array represents how related the entity is to a particular *aspect* or dimension in the space.

The wild thing is that these numbers can tell you how everything is related to everything else. Just numbers!

At the conference, a theory started to form about how we could use a knowledge of how vector embeddings are used to create content that is really good at meeting user intent.

I was sharing this theory with my friend Jane, when Google's Gary Illyes walked by. Jane said, "Ask him about vector embeddings!" I was a little embarrassed to ask a Google engineer about a theory I had only just developed on a topic for which I had very little knowledge. Yet, Jane pulled Gary over and said, "Marie has a question for you."

So, I asked him, "Should I pay attention to understanding vector embeddings?"

He paused for a long time before replying.

Yes. He said I should.

But only because they are interesting. Not because they can help me get an advantage in search.

The next day Gary gave his keynote speech. The timing was perfect because it fell on September 18, 2023, four days into the catastrophic September helpful content update. On this particular day of the update, many websites suffered drastic and lasting declines in traffic. Gary said jokingly not to ask him questions about this update, but instead, he pointed to me in the first row, "Ask Marie."

He said he couldn't stop thinking about my question on vector embeddings. Should we learn about them?

Yes, he said again, but also, **"we should think more like a human when looking at content."**

I want you to keep thinking about this.

Think more like a human when looking at content. In fact, here is a good exercise if you are willing to put this book down and think for a few minutes. Think about your content and ask yourself which parts look good to machines and which parts really look good to humans.

When you're ready, come on back.

Gary said Google is **teaching their algorithms to evaluate content like a human would** and that **vector embeddings are very much the same thing**. **They help Google evaluate content more like a human would, and return results that are more likely helpful for the users.**

He finished by saying, "Publish original, helpful content created for people."

Gary told me I couldn't gain an advantage by learning more about vector embeddings. But I couldn't stop thinking about it. Instead of going to the next session at the conference, I spent the next few hours chatting with ChatGPT about a theory I had on how to optimize content. I very quickly ran a rudimentary test by rewriting some of my content on a page that was struggling to rank.

A few hours later, the page jumped up in rankings for many important keywords.

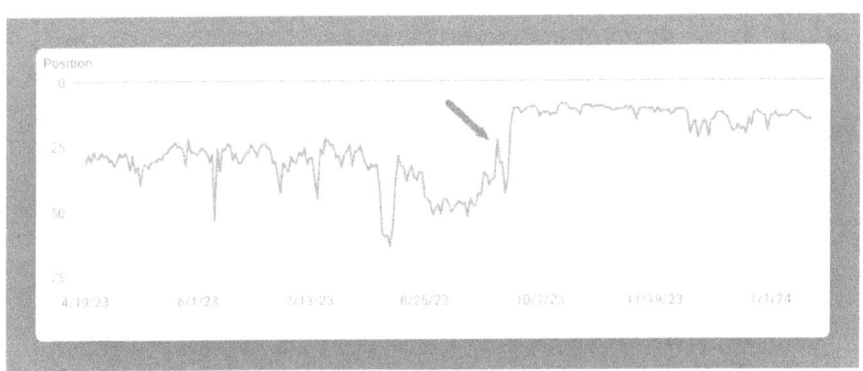

Excited by this discovery, I sent an email to a site I'd been working with and said, "Hey, can I optimize a piece of content for you to test out a theory?"

They gave me full reign to make some changes on a content that was ranking on page three for some competitive medical queries. I put my theory to the test →

1) Understand the user's questions.

2) *Really* understand their intent.

3) Change the content so it better meets that intent and answers the real questions they have.

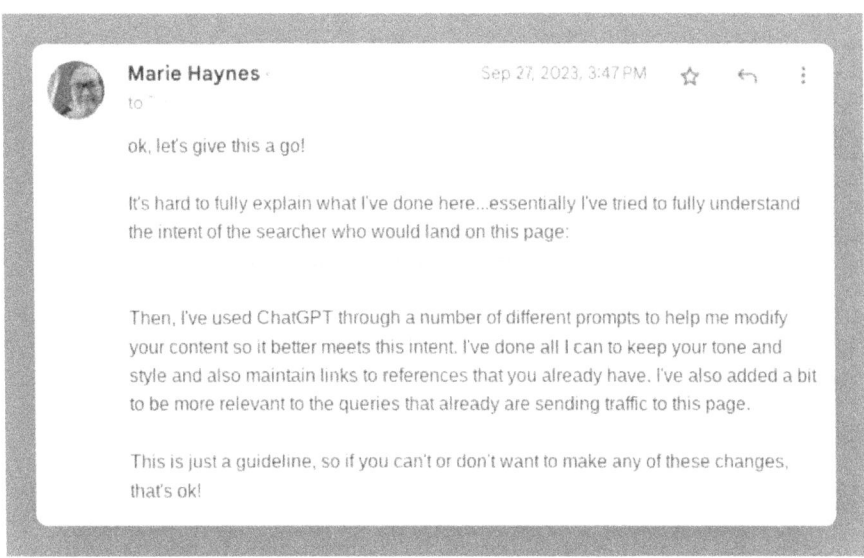

The client made changes September 28th, and well, they made a big difference!

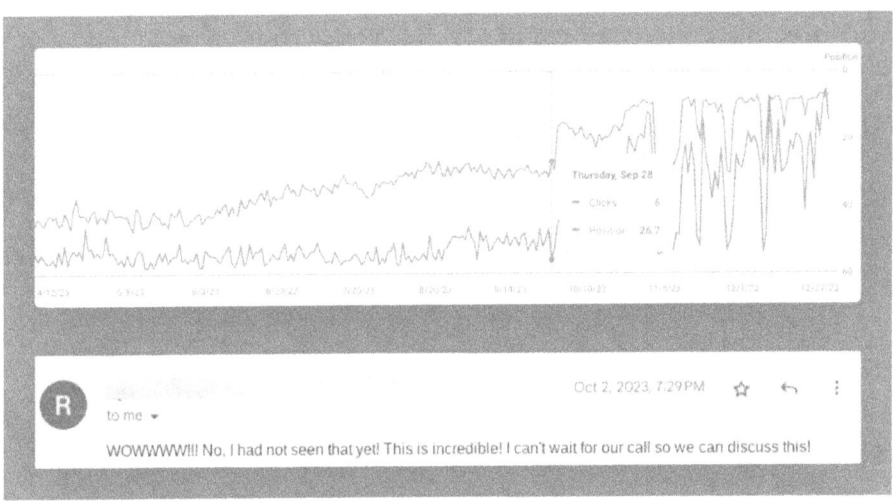

Now, let me get you even more excited about vector embeddings.

Vector embeddings

To understand vector embeddings we need to revisit our high school math. I promise it will not be as complicated as this looks!

Picture a two dimensional graph with x and y coordinates. Any point on this graph can be described by two points. For example, this red dot below sits at a point where x=3 and y=4. Its coordinates are [3,4].

I've used ChatGPT's code interpreter to help me make the images below. The 3d one isn't quite perfect, but hopefully you'll get the idea.

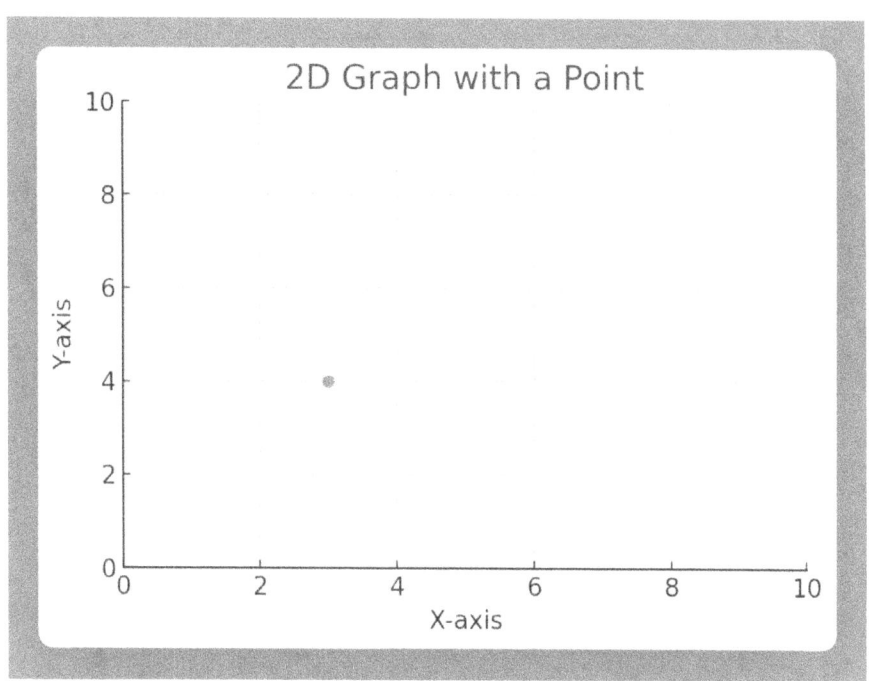

Now let's picture a 3 dimensional graph that has x, y and z coordinates. A point in this space would have 3 coordinates.

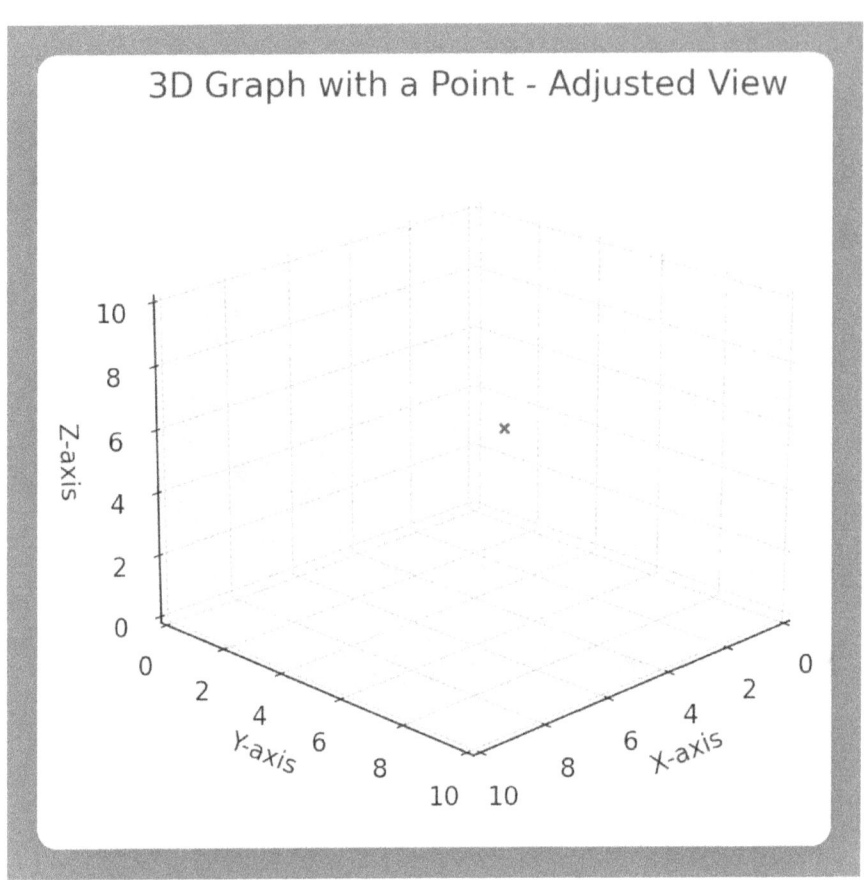

It's hard for our brains to imagine more than 3 dimensions. A vector space that is used by an LLM system like Gemini or ChatGPT may have hundreds or thousands of dimensions.

Each point in that space contains a set of numbers that determine its position. This is called a vector. The numbers in the vector describe some aspect of the features or attributes of the word or token (because it's not always just words) in that space.

For now, let's just think of a 3 dimensional space, where any point in that space can be defined by x, y, and z coordinates. That's all my brain can handle!

Now let's picture that we put words in this space. We're not actually storing words themselves, but we're using a collection of numbers to represent the words. In our 3 dimensional space, each dimension (x, y and z) would represent a characteristic of that word. And together, those characteristics describe the word quite well.

Say we put the word "king" in this space. Our space has dimensions of "maleness"and "royalty". The word "king" is going to sit in a spot in that vector space that shows characteristics that plot it at 100% likely to be related to both maleness and royalty. The word "man", by contrast, has only a small chance of being royal, but is almost certainly likely to be male. The word "woman" again, has a vector that represents that she is very unlikely to be royal, and is also very unlikely to be male.

We can do math with these vectors. Like add them and subtract them and even complicated math with trigonometry to determine how similar certain vectors are.

It turns out that if you take the vector for "king," and you *subtract* the vector for "male," then *add* the vector for "woman" you get really close to...you guessed it, the vector for "queen".

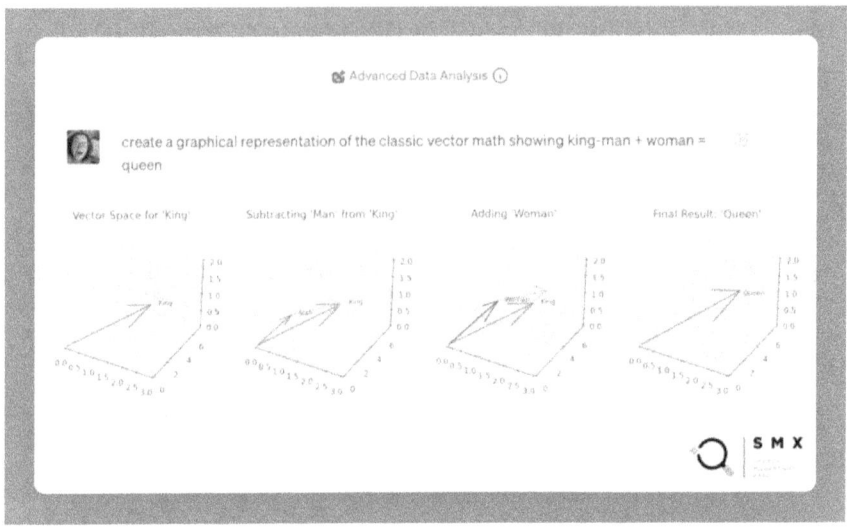

When a large language model produces a response, it leverages these complex vector operations that understand how each word relates to the other words in the sentence, or even in the entire context of what you've discussed in that chat instance.

Transformers

A gigantic breakthrough in AI research happened in 2017 when Google developed, and gave free for everyone to use, something called the Transformer architecture. Transformers help the language model know where to focus its attention in its vast vector space of information it could access.

The transformer architecture is what allows the model to not just randomly predict words from its entire lexicon, but rather, know which words are likely to be relevant and worth paying attention to.

Every AI tool you use today, including ChatGPT, is built on Google's transformer architecture.

And more recently in February of 2024, Google came out with an even more revolutionary architecture that will make their AI faster, more efficient and more accurate, a version of something called a Mixture of Experts architecture. We'll talk shortly about how Gemini 1.5 with its new type of MoE architecture greatly improves Google's AI game, and along with it, Google's ability to understand intent and which content meets that intent.

Transformers lead to a breakthrough in natural language processing called BERT.

BERT

It is worth spending time reading the paper behind Google's language model, BERT[35].

Once again, Google released this technology for all to use.[36] Prior to this, one of the biggest struggles in the field of using AI to understand language was the shortage of training data. For a deep learning system to be best trained, you need massive amounts of training data. BERT introduced a set of

---

[35] BERT: Pre-training of Deep Bidirectional Transformers for Language Understanding. Google. 11 Oct, 2018. https://arxiv.org/pdf/1810.04805.pdf

[36] Open Sourcing BERT: State-of-the-Art Pre-training for Natural Language Processing. Google Research Blog. 2 Nov, 2018. https://blog.google/products/search/search-language-understanding-bert/

training data that people could use that was pre-trained on enormous amounts of text from BooksCorpus and Wikipedia.

The new thing that BERT introduced was the idea of **context**. In previous word embedding models, the word "bank" in the phrases "bank account" and "bank of the river" might be treated the same. But with BERT, each word is treated in the context of the entire sentence so it can understand that the bank of a river is a completely different concept than a bank account.

I find the idea of context fascinating. When we engage in a conversation with someone, our brain works tirelessly to comprehend the gist of what that person is saying. We don't memorize every word they are saying. Rather, we understand the *context* of the conversation and use that to make sense of the individual words.

LLMs work in a similar way.

One of the breakthroughs in understanding the context of words was BERT.

In October of 2019, Google announced BERT, telling us this technology helped it "understand searches better than ever before[37]".

---

[37] Understanding searches better than ever before. Google. The Keyword Blog. 25 Oct, 2019. https://blog.google/products/search/search-language-understanding-bert/

BERT is really good at understanding the **intent behind a query**, or in other words, what the searcher is really trying to accomplish.

BERT gets even more accurate when it is fine tuned for use for a specific purpose. And oh, hey. Google has a version of BERT that's fine-tuned for a specific purpose. It's called RankEmbed BERT.

How it is fine-tuned is of great interest to us!

Fine-tuning

Fine-tuning can take a pre-trained model, such as BERT or GPT, and customize it to be better used for a particular task. This is done by showing the model example after example that is representative of the task that it wants to learn.

Say a model was being trained to understand the sentiment of a review. You might feed it examples like this that are labeled as either positive or negative in terms of sentiment:

Review	Sentiment
I love these headphones. The sound quality is amazing.	Positive
Very disappointed with this purchase. The product stopped working in a week.	Negative

Over time, and especially with a large number of reviews, you are teaching the system to recognize when a review is likely to be positive or negative

Or, let's say you were fine-tuning a model that was trying to predict whether an email was spam. You might give it examples that look like this:

Email text	Label
Meeting rescheduled to 3pm on Thursday	Not spam
Congratulations! You've won a cruise to Mexico!	Spam

The more examples the model is fed, the better it gets at being able to predict whether an email is likely to be spam or not.

The same can be done with question and answer models. You can give it examples of questions that are answered accurately and questions that are inaccurate.

As the model sees these it looks at what its answer would have been to each question and calculates how far its prediction is from the correct answer. It is able to adjust the weights so that its answers are more likely to be closer to the answer it should have given.

It's not like the model is saying, "Oh, I see, when you ask this question you want this exact answer." Rather, it's getting a little bit better at understanding the complexities of that topic or perhaps of how it was communicated, and producing an answer that's likely to be helpful.

What is important for us to know is that a complex model needs to see a **lot of examples** to get the most out of fine-tuning. Like a LOT.

RankEmbed BERT

Google has their own version of BERT that is specifically fine-tuned so as to help improve rankings, RankEmbed BERT. We talked about RankEmbed BERT in the schema section of this book. It's one of the deep learning systems talked about in the Pandu Nayak testimony in the DOJ trial against Google.

RankEmbed is used as a part of the retrieval process - the process where Google's systems figure out which documents are likely to contain information that is relevant to a query.

> **A.** Some of the deep learning systems are also involved in the retrieval process, like we discussed, like the RankEmbed system.
>
> **Q.** Yes, but --
>
> **A.** But unless we retrieve the right documents, you can't score them, yes.
>
> **Q.** But most of the retrieval process happens under the core system, right?
>
> **A.** Other than, as I said, the RankEmbed thing also does retrieval.
>
> **THE COURT:** I'm sorry, you said RankEmbed?
>
> **THE WITNESS:** Yes. RankEmbed bought one of those deep learning systems that also does retrieval.

RankEmbed BERT is trained on click and query data from the web. It's a model that learns from what people are clicking on and then uses that knowledge to predict what people click on.

As quality raters rate query sets for Google, they help Google determine whether the new predicted algo is an improvement on the old.

The ratings of the raters produce a score for Google called IS - information satisfaction. As we discussed in the previous section, this info fine-tunes the RankEmbed BERT model so that it is continually improving on matching queries with relevant results.

> Q. And I'm not going to say the percentage, because I think that those are off limits, but RankEmbed BERT is trained on click and query data, right?
> A. Yes, it is.
> Q. And then it's fine-tuned on human IS rater data?
> A. Yes, it is.

Soooo.....let's put all of this together.

BERT is a model, like a language model similar to GPT, that is trained to understand the connections between words.

BERT can be fine-tuned for specific uses.

RankEmbed BERT is a version of BERT that is *specifically fine-tuned* to help Google better predict which content is likely to meet the need of a searcher who typed this query.

RankEmbed BERT was trained by click and query data to understand what it is that people are finding relevant and helpful.

It is fine-tuned by the feedback of the quality raters.

In the course we talk about this in more detail and also talk more about another system, one called DeepRank. It uses this same BERT technology combined with studying what people search for to deepen its understanding of the world.

We'll also talk about Instant Glue which is a fascinating system that learns what is relevant by studying what people click on.

Phew…ok, that was exciting, but how does that help us create content that meets user intent? To understand this we need to get even more geeky. I'm sorry. It will all make sense soon.

What happens when keywords are replaced by attributes?

I know I told you not to think about search engines, but we need to for just a little bit so that we can understand how Google finds content that is likely to be relevant to a query.

Once we understand how a query is interpreted, or actually, modified, by Google, then we can use our knowledge of vector embeddings to determine what type of content Google would consider to be a good relevant match to that query.

Whenever I read a search patent, I think of the late Bill Slawski who did so much for our industry's understanding of search. If you want to learn more about how search works, you will find endless fascinating reading on his blog at SEO by the Sea[38] as Bill has dissected countless Google patents and papers.

A few days before Bill passed away, I had invited him to be a guest on my podcast.

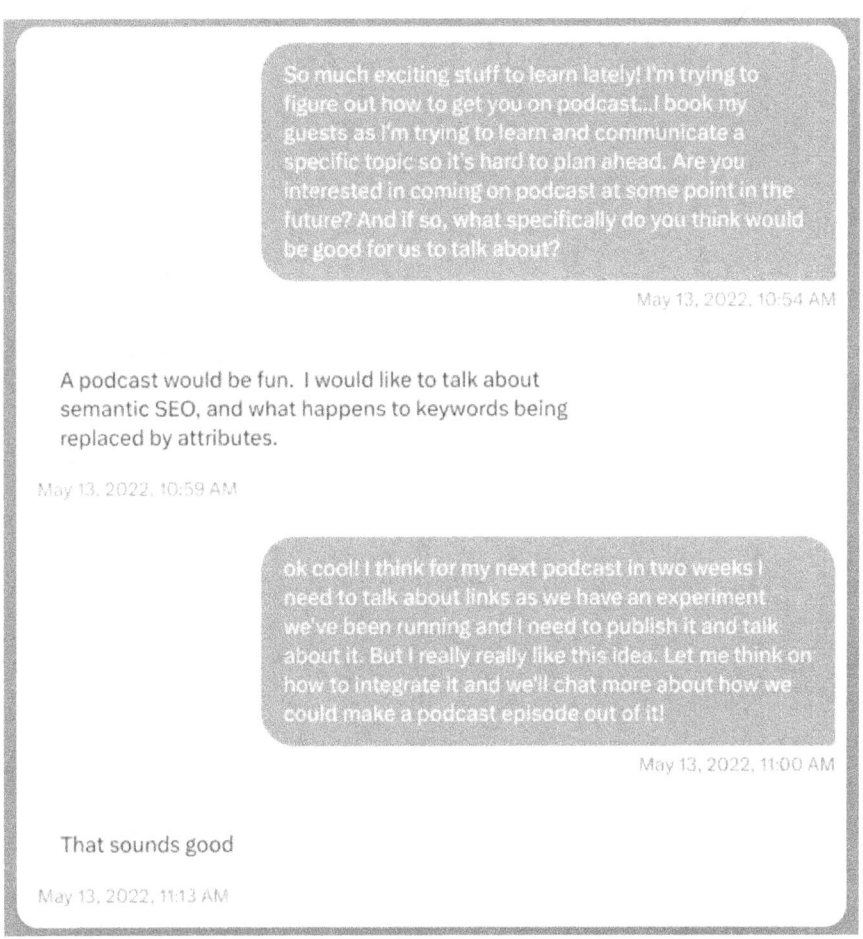

He wanted to talk about what happens when keywords are replaced by attributes. I read his article several times, but it wasn't until I was able to understand more about language models and embeddings that it fully clicked just how important this is.

---

[38] SEO by the Sea. Bill Slawski. https://www.seobythesea.com/

I would recommend pausing here to read Bill's last blog post, Identifying Subjective Attributes of Entities[39].

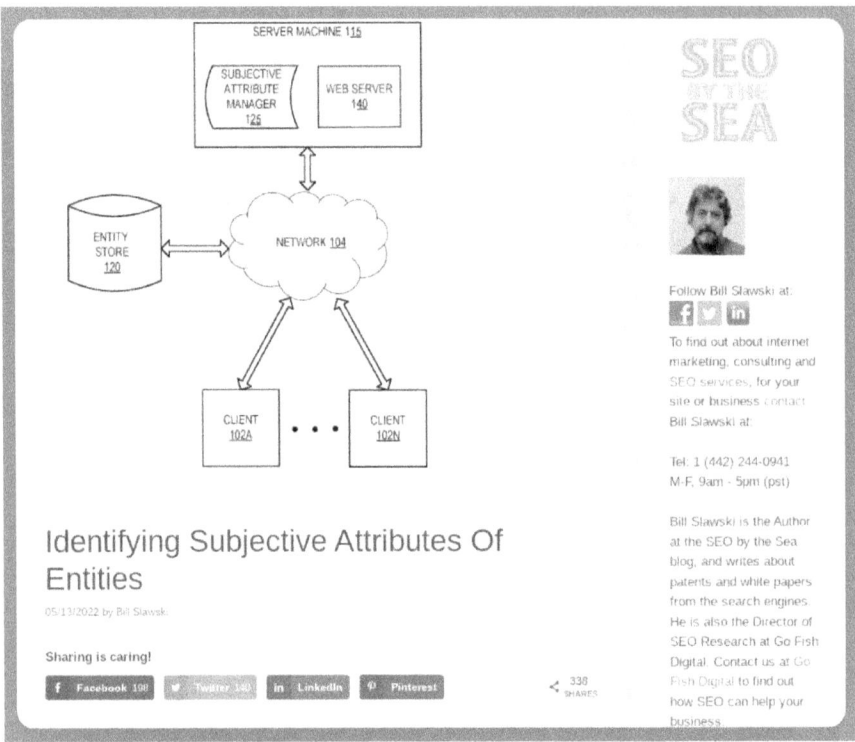

The paper he is describing talks about how search engines can determine which *attributes* are important when we are talking about an entity.

It turns out you can learn a lot about something by looking at what words people use when they talk about it. Say the word "cute" is used often to describe a particular video shared on

---

[39] Identifying Subjective Attributes of Entities. Bill Slawski. May 2022. https://www.seobythesea.com/2022/05/identifying-subjective-attributes-of-entities/

social media. Then, "cute" is an *attribute* that likely describes that video. So now when someone is searching for a cute video, this one is more likely to appear relevant.

So here's what I've just realized.

Remember how we talked about vectors? Vectors are the information that is stored in a vector space. Each vector is a collection of numbers.

Each number tells the system how related the vector is to certain features or attributes. Think of it like a scorecard, where each score shows how likely it is that a particular feature is present in the data.

For example, if you have a vector that represents a fruit, the numbers in that vector might represent its sweetness, color, and size. A high number for sweetness means the fruit is very sweet. This way, the vector helps the system understand and compare different items based on their characteristics or attributes.

(Chat helped me with that analogy.)

Can you see how exciting this is?

If you can understand what a searcher really is trying to accomplish and your content demonstrates those attributes, it will be more likely to look connected to other content on topics in this vector space. And it will be more likely to be seen as similar to a searcher's query.

Now, there clearly is much more that can be said on this topic. We have a lot of learning to do.

I would encourage you to read the following papers. You can upload the PDF download of these papers to ChatGPT or Bard, or copy the information in, and ask questions of it, like

Please explain this paper to me briefly

What does this information tell us about how Google ranks results?

Efficient Estimation of Word Representations in Vector Space[40]. This Google paper talks about how words are represented in a vector space.

Find anything blazingly fast with Google's vector search technology[41]. This article talks about the technology behind vector search used at Google for image search, YouTube, Google play "and more", for "billions of recommendations and information retrievals for Google users worldwide. I expect that "and more" might refer to the re-ranking of the top 20-30 results that is done with RankBrain.

---

[40] Efficient Estimation of Word Representations in Vector Space. Mikolov, Chen, Corrado, Dean. Jan 2016. https://arxiv.org/abs/1301.3781

[41] Find anything blazingly fast with Google's vector search technology. Google Cloud Blog. December 2021. https://cloud.google.com/blog/topics/developers-practitioners/find-anything-blazingly-fast-googles-vector-search-technology

> **Vector Search: the technology behind Google Search, YouTube, Play, and more**
>
> How can it find matches that fast? The trick is that the MatchIt Fast demo uses the vector similarity search (or nearest neighbor search or simply vector search) capabilities of the Vertex AI Matching Engine, which shares the same backend as Google Image Search, YouTube, Google Play, and more, for billions of recommendations and information retrievals for Google users worldwide. The technology is one of the most important components of Google's core services, and not just for Google: it is becoming a vital component of many popular web services that rely on content search and information retrieval accelerated by the power of deep neural networks.

This document tells us how vector search differs from traditional information retrieval. They say, "Vector search provides a much more refined way to find content, with subtle nuances and meanings."

> In contrast, vector search uses vectors (where each vector is a list of numbers) for representing and searching content. The combination of the numbers defines similarity to specific topics. For example, if an image (or any content) includes 10% of "movie", 2% of "music", and 30% of "actor"-related content, then you could define a vector [0.1, 0.02, 0.3] to represent it. (Note: this is an overly simplified explanation of the concept; the actual vectors have much more complex vector spaces). You can find similar content by comparing the distances and similarities between vectors. This is how Google services find valuable content for a wide variety of users worldwide in milliseconds.

<u>Nearest neighbor search</u>[42]. This Wikipedia article is recommended by Google in the previous blog post.

<u>Announcing ScaNN: Efficient Vector Similarity Search</u>[43]. This system helped Google get even better at figuring out which vectors are relevant to a search.

---

[42] Nearest neighbor search. Wikipedia.
https://en.wikipedia.org/wiki/Nearest_neighbor_search#Approximate_nearest_neighbor
[43] Announcing ScaNN: Efficient Vector Similarity Search. Philip Sun. Google

Simplifying all of this

That was a lot to learn. I've spent so many hours digesting these papers and articles and still feel I could spend hundreds more.

We know that Google's AI System RankBrain, re-ranks the top 20-30 results for every search. Or at least it was that number when the DOJ vs Google trial happened. The number may have changed as Google's computational abilities continue to improve. While I have speculated on how it does that, we know that the goal of this system is to return to the searcher something they are likely to find relevant and helpful.

So, while it is incredibly interesting to learn how these different systems work, ultimately our goals are quite simple.

How do you know what the intents and microintents of your audience are?

In the course, we walk through understanding the intent of a query like BERT does. Once we know how a query is interpreted, we can understand how Google modifies the query to find content that comprehensively meets the micro-

---

Research blog. July 2020. https://blog.research.google/2020/07/announcing-scann-efficient-vector.html

intents of that query. Then, we can create content to directly meet the micro-intents.

If you can do that in a way that incorporates your real world experience and unique enthusiasm for your topics then chances are really good for you to see ranking improvements.

So far we have learned about understanding and meeting searcher need, and we've got a basic idea of what topics and subtopics should be covered to improve our chances of Google's vector search as calculating that our content is closely related and relevant to the searcher's needs. We've also considered building out our topical authority on our content by creating hubs and spokes of content.

But there is more.

Google wants to reward content that people find helpful, original and insightful. We can use AI to *help us brainstorm on how to produce this*, but ideally, these ideas need to come from you! What will set your content apart is your real world experience and knowledge on what is topical and important to your audience right now.

Understanding and meeting user intent will help us create relevant content. But we still need to talk about **effort, helpfulness, information gain, demonstrating experience, and very importantly, developing a reputation for being known as a helpful source where people go for more on your topics.**

Part 2: People-First Content

Effort

The word, "effort" is mentioned 99 times in the most recent version of Google's quality raters' guidelines.

Content that is helpful usually is content that has had a lot of effort put into it. Here are a few places where the QRG mentions the importance of effort:

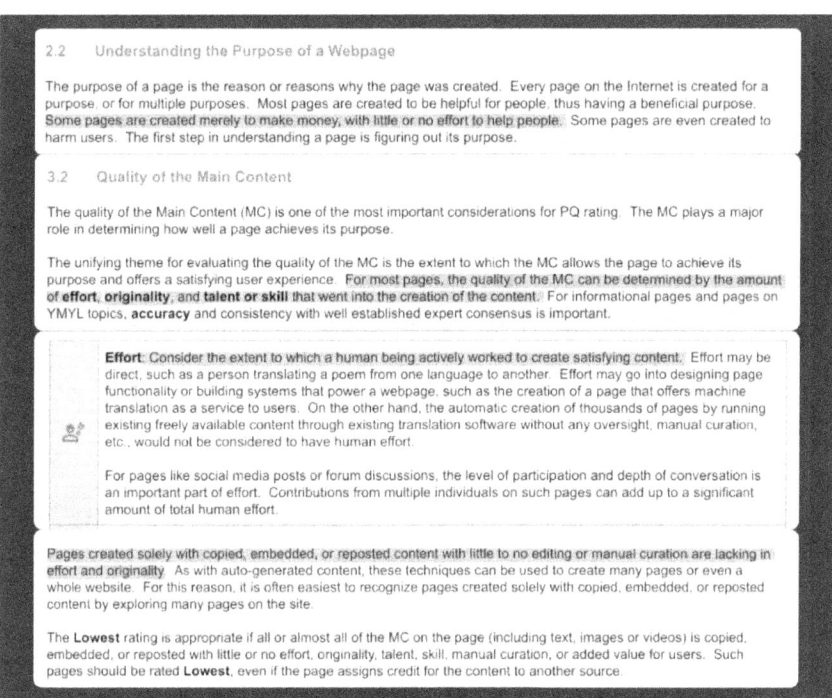

Putting effort into creating content is not the only thing that matters, but today, it is hard to rank content that has not had effort put into it, unless perhaps you are a very well known brand.

I'd encourage you to put most of your effort into learning what it is that your audience wants. Or better yet, what they *need*. **If you can help your audience improve in some way, especially if you can do that in a way that no one else can, you're creating helpful content.**

Audience. The importance of being known for your topics

It is very difficult to create people-first content without first having an audience. Otherwise, you are producing content that you think *search engines will show to people*. There is a big difference.

Understanding this requires a mindset shift for many who have a solid understanding of SEO. We have wired ourselves to do all we can to look good to Google. All this time, Google has silently been shifting more and more to a system that, thanks to AI, learns what looks good to people.

People like to engage with brands. Or with personalities. They generally like websites that they somehow recognize and trust.

Why does Google rank Chapters and Amazon for this search below?

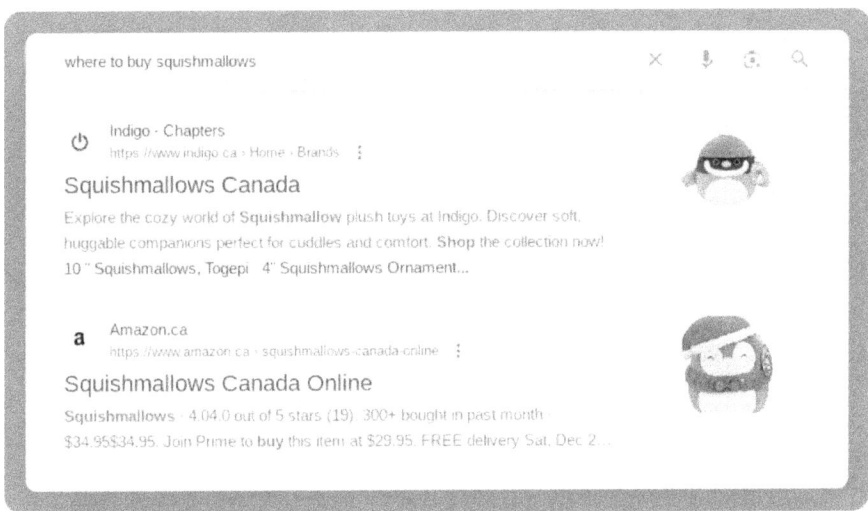

It's because that's where I'd likely buy this product! There was a day when someone with a lot of SEO knowledge could make a site outrank these giant brands. AI has changed this.

AI tries to predict what people will find satisfying, and it has a lot of data to use in these predictions.

Look at this interesting search. It brought up a carousel of what looks to be loads of helpful content.

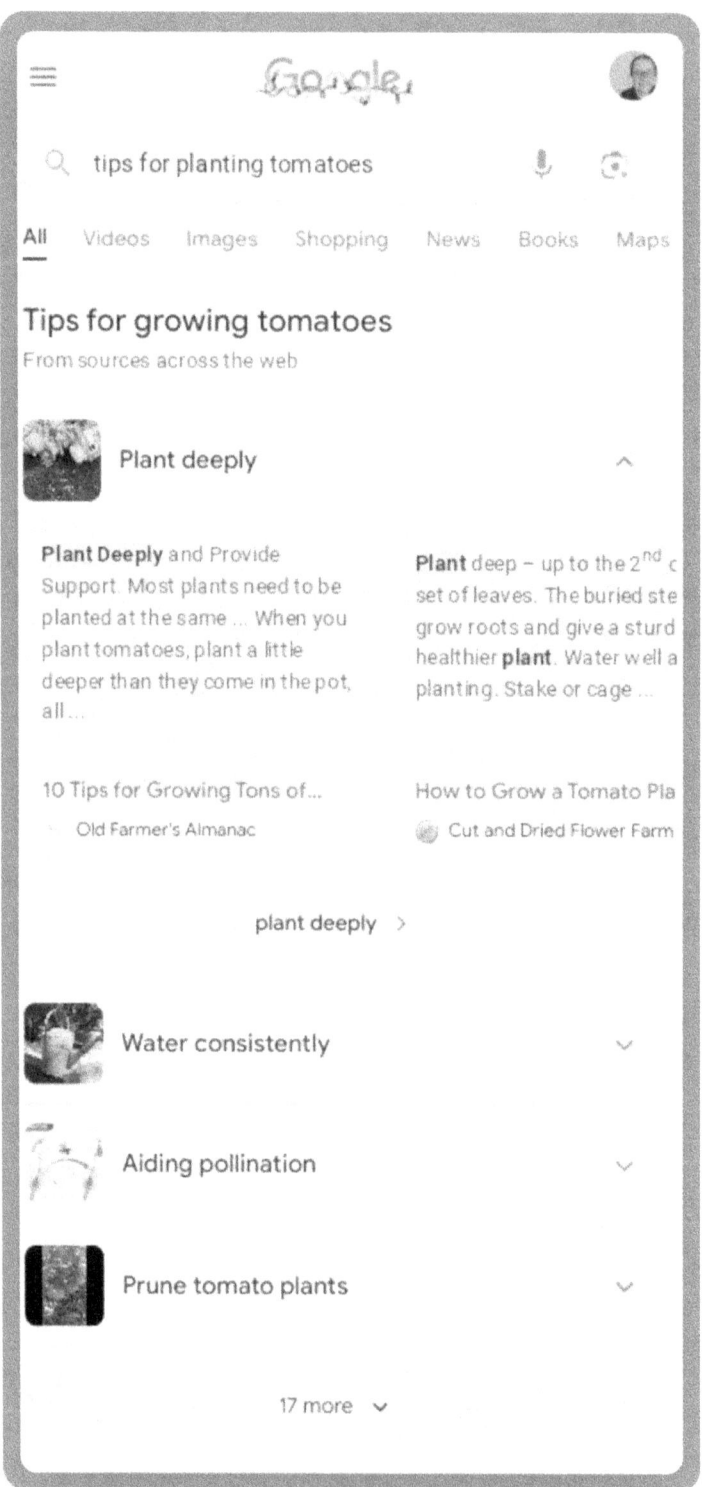

I am seeing results like this more and more. We will talk near the end of this book how AI is allowing Google to create all sorts of modules of helpful content to show searchers, and not just in search. Also in Google assistant which is becoming more and more important.

Each of those dropdowns contains a carousel of websites, all with some type of **reputation for the topic** of growing tomatoes:

- Farmer's Almanac - Known for agriculture
- Cut and Dried Flower Farm - An actual farm that blogs about their experiences, with a store where real people spend money
- Better Homes and Gardens - Known for gardening

And then there's this site. A small blog. A "hidden gem":

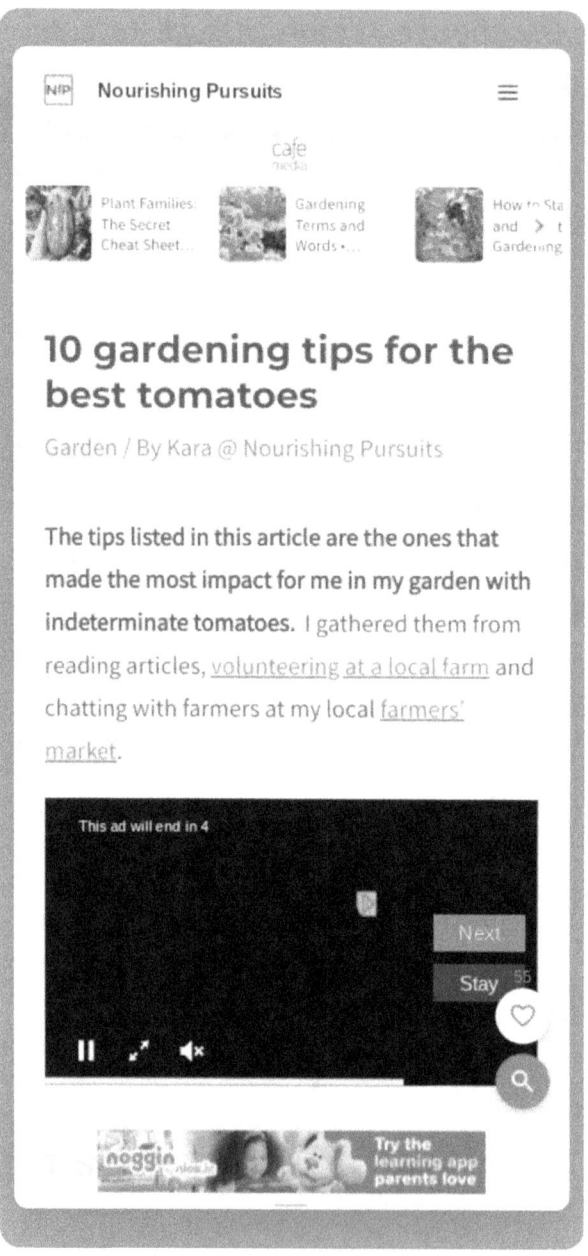

A side note about spam

Is this a hidden gem? A blogger who loves to garden and creates great content? I have not dug deeply to investigate whether this blog legitimately is a small blogger sharing her experiences in gardening or whether this is a new type of sophisticated spam that I am seeing more and more of where blackhats create all the appearances of being a small blogger along with social media profiles and other online hints like mentions on podcast appearances and even in some cases, photoshopped images on Google maps.

You may have sites like this ranking in your niches. They are so good at manipulation, you often cannot tell what is real and what is not.

This type of manipulation I'm talking about is spam, and as we discussed earlier, Google is aware of its rise. We should see significantly less of it as Google's AI systems learn.

Tip: We can learn from what it is that is currently ranking, as we can get clues as to the types of things that Google's systems tend to consider helpful. If you do think you've got spam ranking in your search results, before Google gets rid of the spam, I'd encourage you to spend time analyzing this spam and try to understand *why* Google thinks it is likely to be helpful. What are they offering that users are eating up?

For now, let's assume that this page is legitimately a blogger, known for the topic of tomato gardening.

You may need to build an audience

For many who are reading this book, you likely need to learn how to build your audience and become known for your topics before you can succeed on Google Search. If you have content that truly is the best of its kind and you are not able to rank, you may find that once you build up an audience and a reputation for your topics, you will start to be shown more.

Here's the great news. **I do believe it's possible to build this audience simply by creating fantastic content.** But I don't think many people are actually creating truly FANTASTIC, original and insightful content. Google really wants to find content that is helpful alongside what already exists in the Library. I do think some who are reading this book will go on to find an audience through search.

I challenge you to think of your niche and your content in new ways!

If you can grasp the concept of people-first content, and how it differs from SEO-first, I believe you're on your way to success in being found on Google. This is true of individual small bloggers and businesses alike.

I'd encourage you to take time to read this Google blog post on how Google is now showing more content by people, for people in Search.

The rater guidelines talk extensively about being known for your topics. Here are just a few examples:

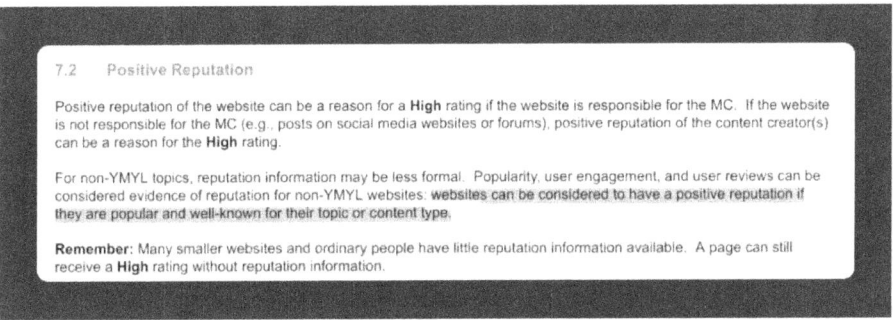

Say you had a website that demonstrated your hand drawn cartoons. You might have the funniest content that is by far what people want to see when they are searching for funny cartoons. But unless you are *known* for the topic of humour, and unless people tend to search you out for your cartoons, you're unlikely to outrank the New Yorker.

Google doesn't know that your cartoons are funny. But they can use signals on the web to discern whether lots of people tend to enjoy your cartoons.

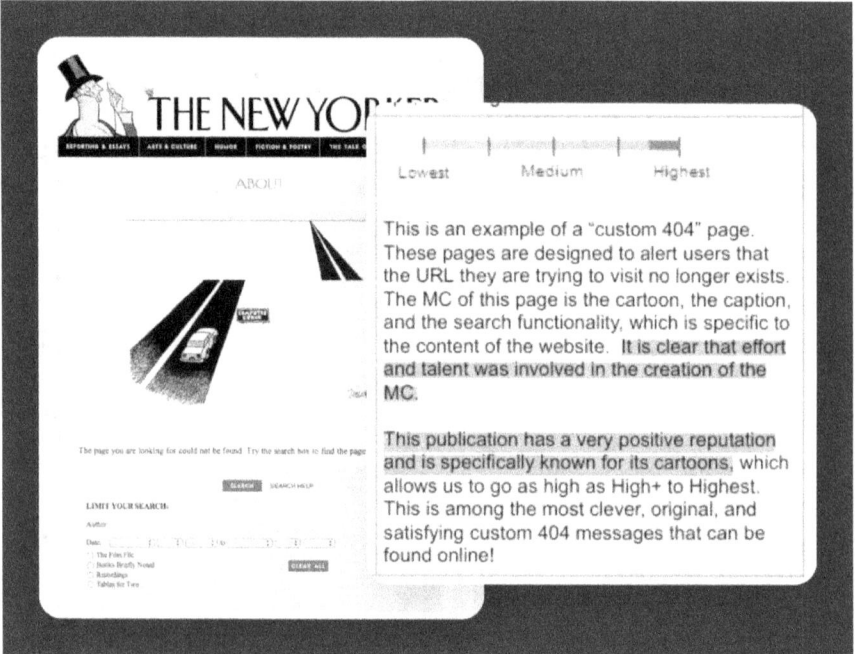

You might have great reviews on tech topics, but it will be difficult to rank against a site like PCMag.com unless you truly can produce content that the machine learning systems predict to be content that people will find more helpful than what exists and click on. If searchers are looking for a list type of article, they're much more likely to click on an authoritative source.

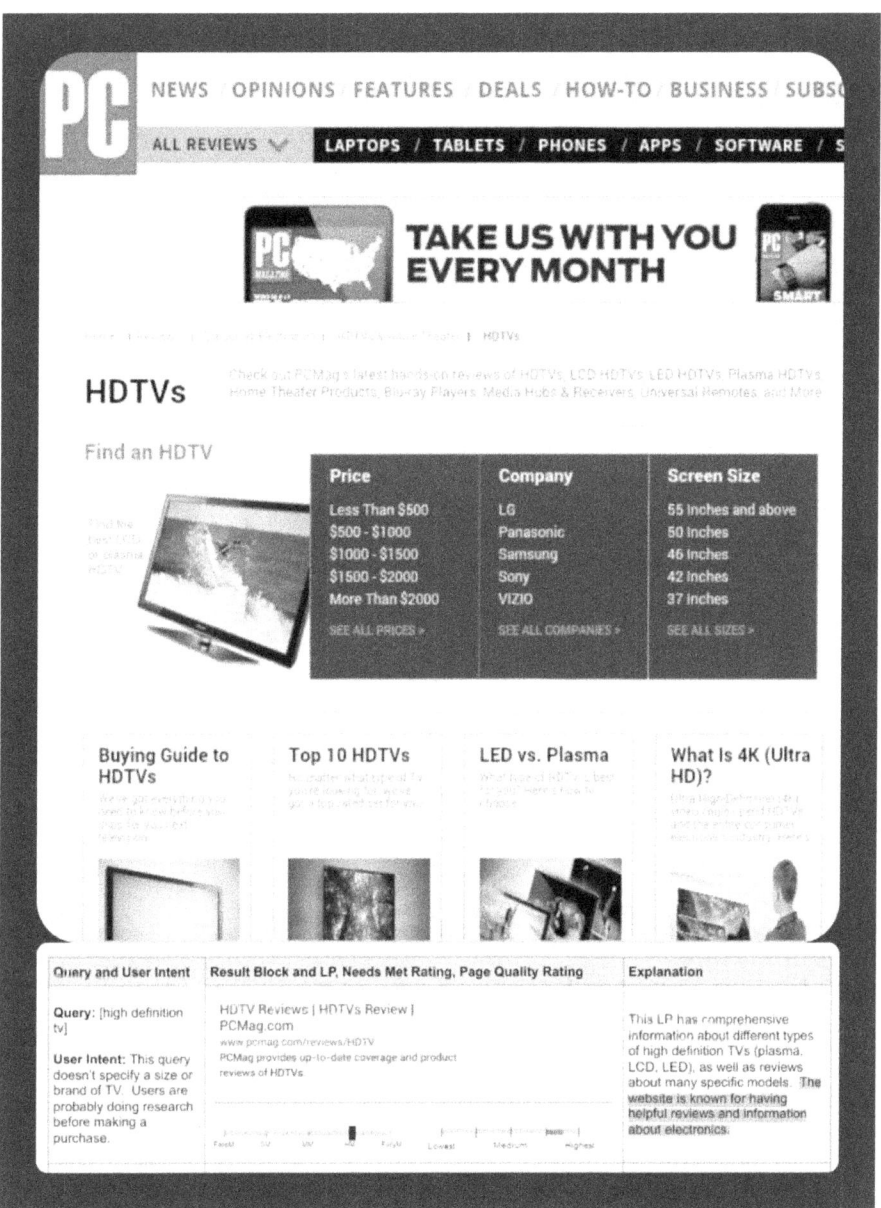

I'd encourage you to really dig around in your SERPs and see if you can find examples of lesser known sites that are ranking amongst the gigantic brands. Brainstorm on what it is that possibly makes the content more helpful. Why did

Google predict that this page is likely to be found helpful by people?

Even better, think bigger than that. I'd encourage you to experiment with creating some kind of content that is *wildly* different from what currently exists. Perhaps no one is doing it because no one is doing it!

We'll brainstorm more ideas on this in a moment.

It would be so cool if you became known for your topic because people were finding you in search and discovering your amazingness. I do believe this can be done. I mean, you found me, right? It might not have been directly from search, but my body of content I have written on Google's algorithms is what gives me the authority to be considered an expert whose book is worth spending this much time reading.

How do you become known?

One of the most quoted phrases about how Google determines EEAT comes from a question I [asked Google employee Gary Illyes](#) at a conference in 2018.

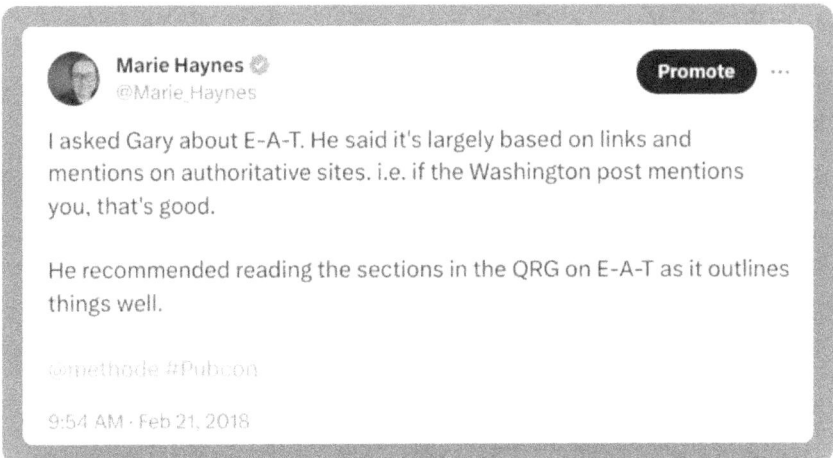

Links are one of the *many* signals that can be used to help Google determine which brands, content creators or even content itself are known for their topics. If we study the rater guidelines and Google's documentation, we can surmise that all of the following possibly could provide Google with signals indicating that the world considers a business as popular and known for their topics:

- **Links** from other sites and people who are known for this topic. Especially links from authoritative places.
- **Mentions** from others known as topic experts. Most likely, even without directly being linked, mentions in authoritative places can help send signals that do more to help Google understand that your content on this topic is worth considering in rankings.
- **Actual popularity.** Do people seek you out when learning on your topics? Do people visit your business? Do people tend to buy from you?

- **Public sentiment.** What do people tend to say about you or your brand in reviews, comments, articles and forums?
- **Social media involvement**, especially if it involves community.
- **Mentions in forums** and other discussions on your topics.
- **Comments around the web.** What do people say about you? Is it obvious that you are known as a source of information for your topics?
- **The content you create.** If you are producing content that truly is original and insightful, especially if you produce a lot of content on a subject, you can show Google that you have a depth of knowledge on a subject.

Here's something you can try. I had better success doing this in ChatGPT, but you may find Gemini gives you good results as well:

You
based on comments left around the web, what is marie haynes known for?

ChatGPT
Marie Haynes is widely recognized for her expertise in understanding Google's search algorithms. She has been working in the SEO field since 2008 and is the founder and CEO of Marie Haynes Consulting (MHC). Her work mainly focuses on helping sites recover from penalties and sharing her findings and insights with the SEO community. Haynes is known for her in-depth knowledge and analysis of Google's algorithms and how they affect search rankings. She emphasizes the importance of creating original, helpful content and adapting to the evolving nature of search engines, particularly with the increasing role of AI in Google's search systems. Her expertise is also evident in her discussions about the impact of Google's Panda algorithm and the significance of links in SEO strategies [11] [11] [11].

You
what topics is she known for

ChatGPT
Marie Haynes is known for her expertise in several key areas within the field of SEO:

1. **Google's Search Algorithms**: She is highly regarded for her deep understanding of Google's search algorithms. Her work often involves analyzing these algorithms and explaining their impacts on website rankings and SEO strategies.
2. **Penalty Recovery**: Haynes has a strong background in helping websites recover from Google penalties. This includes addressing issues that lead to penalties and providing strategies for recovery.
3. **Helpful Content and AI in SEO**: She emphasizes the importance of creating original and helpful content that aligns with Google's evolving search algorithms. Haynes discusses the integration of AI in search, like Google's Helpful Content System, and how it's reshaping the internet and SEO practices.
4. **SEO Strategies and Trends**: Haynes is known for her insights into effective SEO strategies and staying ahead of the curve with emerging trends in the industry.
5. **Content Quality and Engagement**: She often speaks about the importance of content quality, engagement, and how to make content more useful and relevant to users.
6. **Links and Link Building**: Haynes has delved into the importance of links in SEO, discussing how they affect website rankings and the evolution of link-building strategies.
7. **SEO Industry Leadership**: As the CEO of Marie Haynes Consulting, she plays a leading role in the SEO community, contributing through her podcasts, newsletters, and social media presence, where she shares her theories and thoughts on Google and SEO [11]

If you do this for your brand and find that you are not known for your topics then you may have work to do! However, keep in mind that often LLMs are slow to divulge information about people as they are still learning what is and isn't acceptable to say. If the LLM doesn't know you, it may just be that they are being careful in providing responses about people.

This brings us to our next GPT in the course. I built this reputation builder brainstormer to generate ideas on how you or your client can become better known. The knowledge base contains loads of my ideas that I've brainstormed with clients in the past (anonymized of course.)

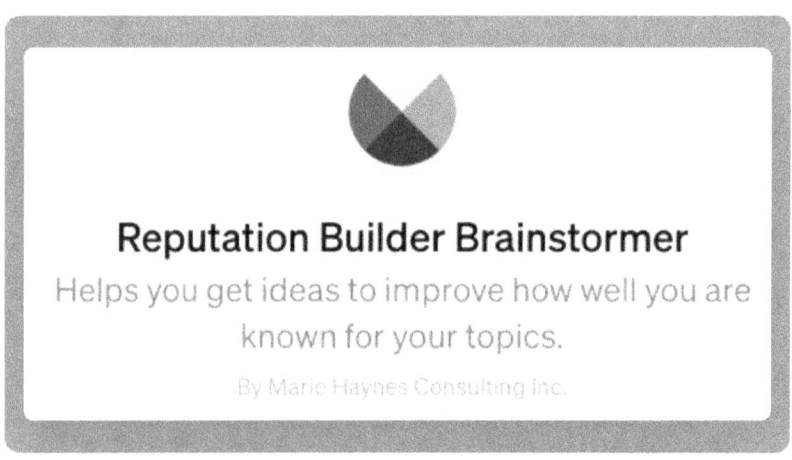

> **You**
> give me specific ideas for improving how well known I am for writing on the topic of the helpful content system
>
> **Reputation Builder Brainstormer**
> To become better known for writing about Google's Helpful Content System, here are five specific strategies you can implement:
>
> 1. **Conduct and Publish Original Research**: Carry out an in-depth study or analysis of how the Helpful Content System has impacted various websites and their search rankings. For example, you could analyze a set of websites before and after a major update to the system, documenting changes in their traffic and ranking. Publish this research with detailed findings and insights on your website and consider submitting it to reputable industry publications for wider reach.
> 2. **Host Webinars and Online Workshops**: Organize and host webinars or online workshops focused on understanding and adapting to the Helpful Content System. Invite other SEO experts to participate and share their insights. These sessions can be a mix of teaching, Q&A, and discussion of real-world cases. Promote these events through social media, industry forums, and email newsletters to attract a wide audience.
> 3. **Create a Comprehensive Guide or E-Book**: Write an extensive guide or e-book on Google's Helpful Content System, offering actionable advice, strategies for compliance, and predictions about future updates. Make this guide available for free download on your website in exchange for email subscriptions, which can help you build a mailing list for future content promotion.
> 4. **Collaborate with Industry Influencers and Podcasts**: Reach out to influencers in the

Once you have an audience you know what content to create because a hungry audience always has needs you can satisfy with fantastic content.

Freshness

In a moment we will discuss improving upon the content you currently have on your site. Ultimately though if you want to produce content that is helpful, you will need to create **new** content that is original and insightful.

I found it interesting that Google recently updated their guidance on helpful content to add information about trying to cheat their freshness system. "Are you changing the date of pages to make them seem fresh when the content has not substantially changed?"

Several of Google's ranking systems are designed to show fresh content for queries *where users are likely to expect it*.

> **Freshness systems**
>
> We have various "query deserves freshness" systems designed to show fresher content for queries where it would be expected. For example, if someone is searching about a movie that's just been released, they probably want recent reviews rather than older articles from when production began. For another example, ordinarily a search for "earthquake" might bring back material about preparation and resources. However, if an earthquake happened recently, then news articles and fresher content might appear.

I believe that freshness has become even more important lately. It makes sense. Let's say I want to be known for the topic of understanding Google updates. My audience is not searching for information to define what a Google update is, or general information on how core updates have worked in the past. There is so much information on this already written on the web. **They want the most current thoughts and examples of recoveries, strategies that they can implement.** They want something that actually helps them.

I challenge you to throw away your current ideas about how to do keyword research. So much of what SEOs do for keyword research is causing us to produce content that is essentially the same as content that Google already has, or content that they can generate with AI! We do keyword research to determine what other people are making and then try to make something slightly better. Or, we do keyword research to determine what Google's People Also Ask Results are to get content ideas when Google **already has content to answer those questions!**

Unless you can produce content that searchers are likely to find **substantially more valuable** than what currently exists for your topics, you are sending more signals to Google to tell them that your content is mediocre and not something they should be hungrily crawling and consuming.

Here are are a few of the helpful content questions that speak to the type of content Google tells us their systems are built to reward:

- Does the content provide original information, reporting, research, or analysis?

- Does the content provide insightful analysis or interesting information that is beyond the obvious?
- If the content draws on other sources, does it avoid simply copying or rewriting those sources, and instead provide substantial additional value and originality?

- Is this the sort of page you'd want to bookmark, share with a friend, or recommend?

- Would you expect to see this content in or referenced by a printed magazine, encyclopedia, or book?
- Does the content provide substantial value when compared to other pages in search results?

- Does your content clearly demonstrate first-hand expertise and a depth of knowledge (for example, expertise that comes from having actually used a product or service, or visiting a place)?

- Are you mainly summarizing what others have to say without adding much value?
- Are you writing about things simply because they seem trending and not because you'd write about them otherwise for your existing audience?
- Does your content leave readers feeling like they need to search again to get better information from other sources?

One of the ways we can help make our content stand out is by continually providing fresh information on our topics.

This might mean updating already published posts to add information that answers new questions that have arisen on a topic. Or, if you have enough to say about a fresh event regarding your topics, you may find this is good information to add a standalone article that acts as a spoke in your hub and spoke wheel.

Hidden Gems

Despite Google's preference to often rank authoritative brands, you do not always need to be a gigantic brand to be known for your topics. Google tells us that they are working to identify and show more hidden gems in search results. These are pages that often live in an [unexpected or hard to find place](#) such as "post on a little-known blog" or an "article with unique expertise on a topic."

> **How we help you find the expertise you need**
>
> In addition to making it easier to find authentic perspectives, we're also improving how we rank results in Search overall, with a greater focus on content with unique expertise and experience. Last year, we launched the helpful content system to show more content made for people, and less content made to attract clicks. In the coming months, we'll roll out an update to this system that more deeply understands content created from a personal or expert point of view, allowing us to rank more of this useful information on Search.
>
> Helpful information can often live in unexpected or hard-to-find places: a comment in a forum thread, a post on a little-known blog, or an article with unique expertise on a topic. Our helpful content ranking system will soon show more of these "hidden gems" on Search, particularly when we think they'll improve the results.

Hidden gems may appear in several places in search. I expect that soon what I write in this workbook will be dated. The search results are changing regularly, giving us glimpses of places where helpful content is featured.

Here are a few places that look to me like they are recognizing the type of content that aligns with what Google says they want to reward. The websites and people listed in here are all known brands or personalities.

We have seen carousels of discussions and forums appear in the search results. What excites me more though is seeing helpful content carousels popping up in carousels, in maps, and even in ads seen in the SGE:

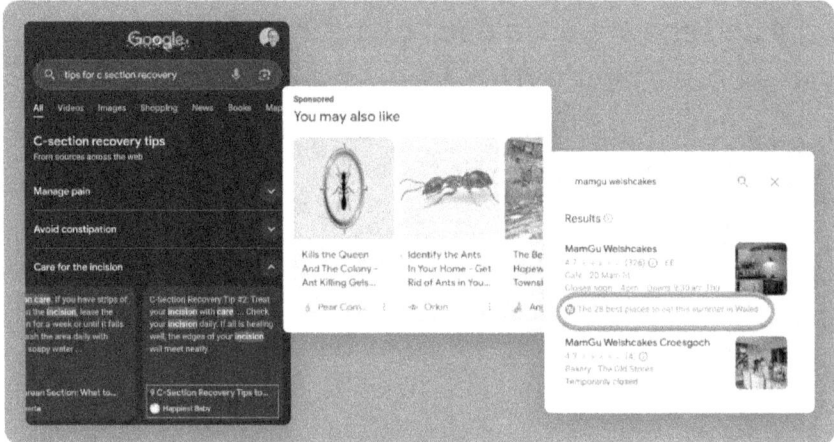

If you are able to create helpful content as described in this book, you should find that you can rank in these places. As Google's systems learn which hidden gems type of content people are finding helpful, you should have even more opportunity. I do expect that Google's systems will continue to improve in recognizing truly helpful gems. I also expect that you will be one of them!

One of the attributes folks were getting excited about in the API files "leak" is smallPersonalSite. I expect this is one of the attributes considered in the machine learning systems that are eager to find and reward Hidden Gems.

Experience

In December of 2022, Google changed the rater guidelines to add more emphasis on experience, saying, "E-A-T gets an extra E for Experience." This update rewarded sites demonstrating real world experience.

The rater guidelines help the raters understand the ideals Google wants their algorithms to reward. In this most recent update, they added a new line under section 2.2: Understanding the Purpose of a Webpage:

> Common helpful or beneficial page purposes include (but are not limited to):
>
> - To share information about a topic.
> - To share a personal experience, perspective, or feelings on a topic.
> - To share pictures, videos, or other forms of media.
> - To demonstrate a personal talent or skill.
> - To express an opinion or point of view.
> - To entertain.
> - To offer products or services.
> - To allow users to post questions for other users to answer.
> - To allow users to share files or to download software.

"To share a personal experience, perspective, or feelings on a topic."

If you were affected by recent Google updates, there is a strong possibility it's related in some way to experience. As you review content that started to outrank yourself, consider how their experience differs from what you have.

What is real world experience?

Here are some examples based on the types of sites I've seen Google start to reward following recent updates.

Sites with customers in the offline world

If you find that the keywords that you used to rank for are now dominated by real world businesses who have customers who pay them money for products or services, you may find these rankings hard to regain.

I think some of these keyword rankings can be re-won by creating content that's significantly more helpful than what the real-world provider has written. I believe some keyword rankings can be regained by creating content that is substantially more informative and valuable than what the current providers have produced.

Known topic experts

The QRG shows example after example of pages that are to be considered high quality because the site is a popular resource for its topic. For example, The Knot is a popular wedding site. The Onion is listed as being known for its humor. I've seen a couple of niche recipe sites impacted by recent updates that had decent content and good recipes, but weren't *known* for any particular thing about their recipes. You might have a great recipe for lamb, but unless there's evidence that people tend to seek you out for your recipes, especially your lamb ones, Google is likely going to show searchers other sites.

I believe some of you who were impacted will be able to recover by learning how to produce content that's so good you become known for your topic.

You have used a product or service

The QRG says,

*"**For some topics, Experience is the most important dimension of Trust.** For other topics, assessing Expertise through the posts may be important."*

This is one of the reasons we are seeing more forum content rank recently. Google's latest QRG update tells us how forum content can demonstrate experience.

> 9.3 Ratings for Forums and Q&A Pages
>
> Ratings for forum and Q&A pages can be challenging. Here is some guidance on how to approach these pages.
>
> - The Main Content includes the question, the answers/responses, and the resulting discussions.
> - Rate from the point of view of a user who visits the page, rather than a participant involved in the discussion.
> - Users who post answers/responses or comments are often identified only by a username or alias. A page can be High or Highest quality with just usernames or aliases depending on other criteria.
> - The E-E-A-T of a discussion among users can often be judged by the posts or comments themselves.
>   - For some topics, Experience is the most important dimension of Trust. For other topics, assessing Expertise through the posts may be important. In some cases, the posters themselves will highlight either their own Experience or Expertise, or other people will comment on it.
>   - Pages on YMYL topics require more attention to Trust and more care in the assessment of E-E-A-T.
> - **Highest quality forum/Q&A pages** have extremely satisfying conversations, including participation from users who have put a great deal of effort into their posts and have a wealth of Experience and/or Expertise on the topic. Such conversations can be very satisfying because of the depth of discussion, the unique insights, or the sharing of experiences that many would not have access to in their real-world community.
> - **Low quality forum/Q&A pages** often lack effort (few responses, surface-level rather than in-depth discussion), lack Experience or Expertise, contain mild inaccuracies, or show a significant lack of respect or decorum among the participants that might deter others from joining the discussion.
> - **Lowest quality forum/Q&A pages** may contain information or advice that is harmfully misleading, contradicts well-established expert consensus, encourages harm towards self or other individuals/participants, etc.

Highest quality forum and Q&A pages *"have extremely satisfying conversations, including participation from users who have put **a great deal of effort** (there's that word again!) **into their posts and have a wealth of Experience and/or Expertise on the topic**. Such conversations can be very satisfying because of the depth of discussion, the unique insights, or the sharing of experiences that many would not have access to in their real-world community."*

If you are an expert in your topic, I believe you can possibly convince Google's systems your content demonstrates real world experience by incorporating more user generated content. More real people talking about you, about your content, about your topics. This may be in the form of helpful comments and discussion or perhaps a well maintained forum.

Your goal should be to get real, insightful conversations going around your topics.

Should you start a forum? It remains to be seen but I think it could be a good idea for some folks. Google recently announced [new structured markup for forums](#) which tells us they want to understand forum content better, and new SERP features to show forum posters in the search results. It seems to me that it is indeed a [good time to have an active forum](#) in your community!

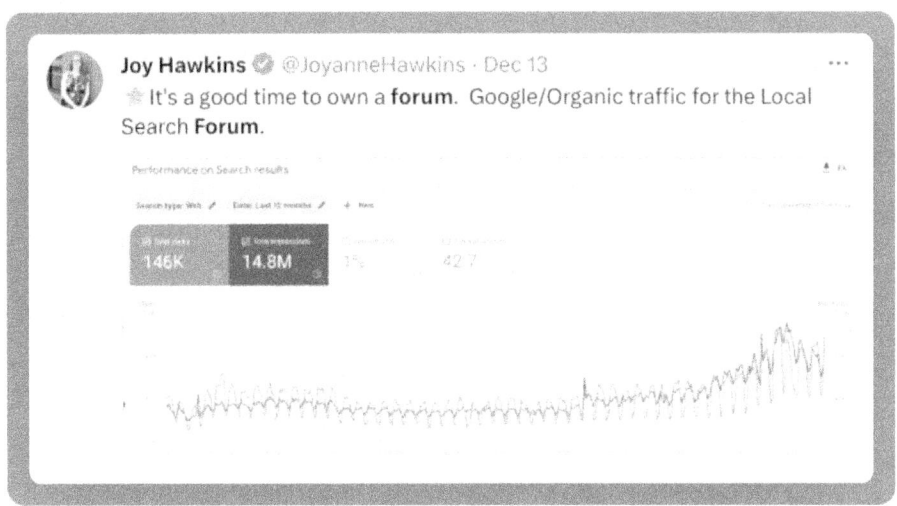

Looking ahead to the future - SGE, Gemini...and AGI?

So far we have discussed how Google's use of AI has already transformed search. There are changes on the horizon that all SEOs should be aware of that are also closely related to AI. Search Generative Experience (SGE), which is now renamed to AI Overviews, and Gemini are already changing how people get their information.

And, if we are to believe Google DeepMind's creator Demis Hassabis[44], within the next decade, Google will achieve their goal - building artificial general intelligence, AGI.

I do believe Demis. And I am excited.

Let's talk first about the immediate changes to the search landscape that every website owner should be aware of. This is a general overview as many of these features and what's important to know about them are changing rapidly. Much of this section will likely be dated by the time you read this book!

---

[44] Demis Hassabis on Chatbots to AGI | EP 71 Hard Fork Podcast. https://www.youtube.com/watch?v=nwUARJeeplA

Google's Search Generative Experience / AI Overviews.

Google's CEO, Sundar Pichai has said that SGE is the future of Search[45].

---

[45] Google's Vision for Search in 2023 and Beyond - Analysis of the 2023 Earnings Call. Marie Haynes. https://www.mariehaynes.com/googles-vision-for-search-in-2023-and-beyond-analysis-of-the-q2-2023-earnings-call/

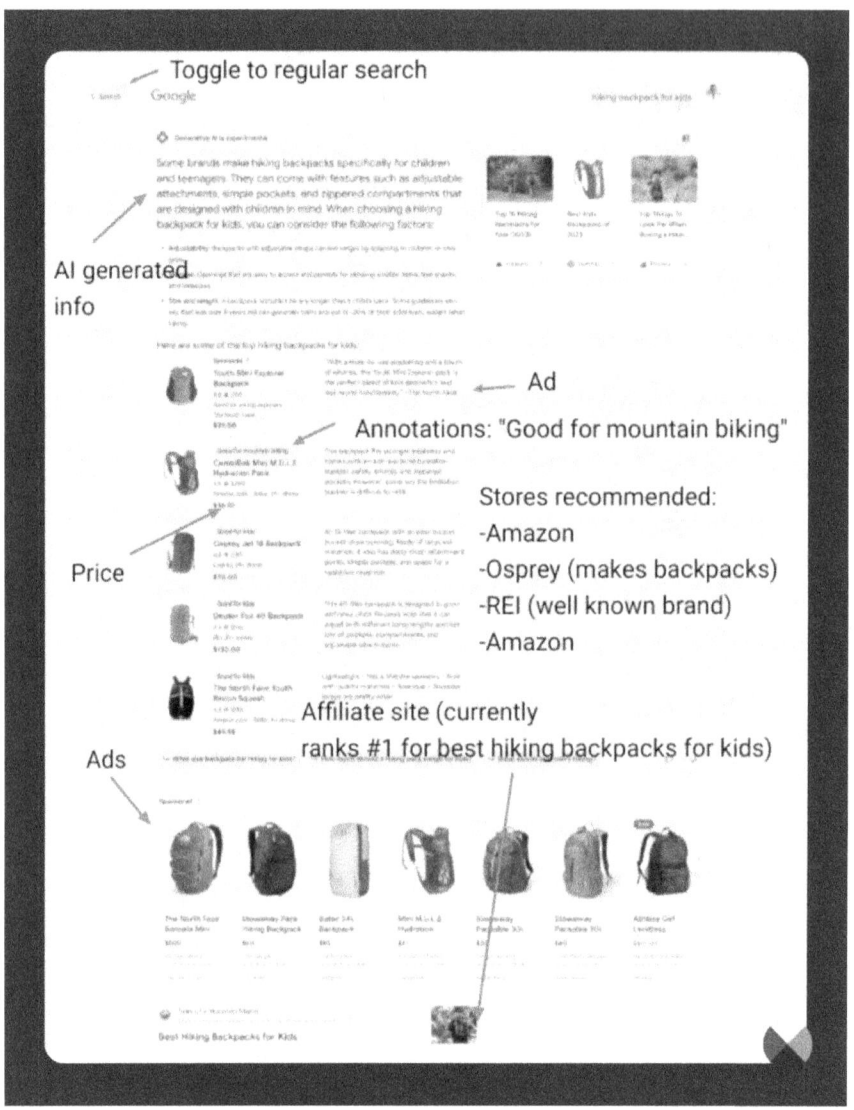

SGE started as an experiment that could be opted into at labs.google.com. This is now in Search in some countries, with a new name, AI Overviews. They can have several different components, or a combination of them, including:

An AI generated answer that appears to be stitched together from multiple websites like a large featured snippet.

Carousels of websites.

I have been calling these "helpful content carousels" because they generally contain the type of content we have been talking about throughout this book. I have since heard them referred to as "link cards." (I like helpful content carousels better!)

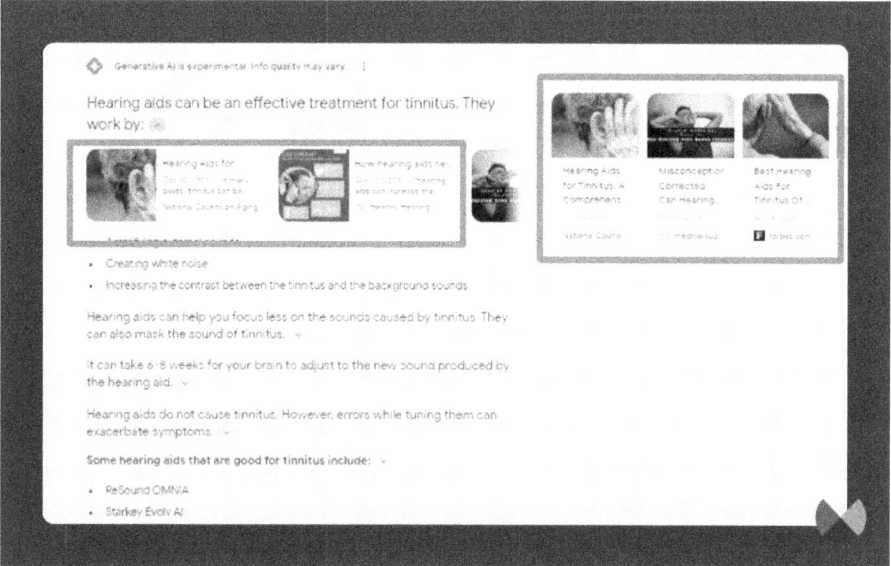

These carousels are appearing in regular searches and also in Google Assistant responses. You may see similar carousels peppered throughout search labeled as "Perspectives", "Forum Discussions", and other labels.

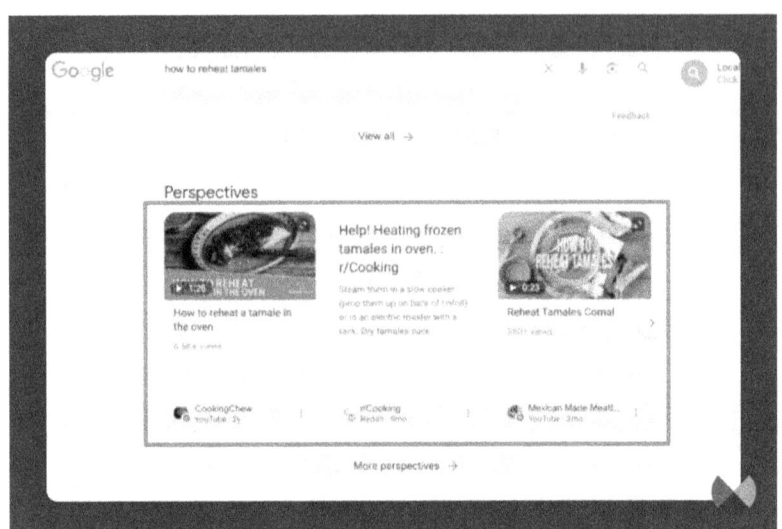

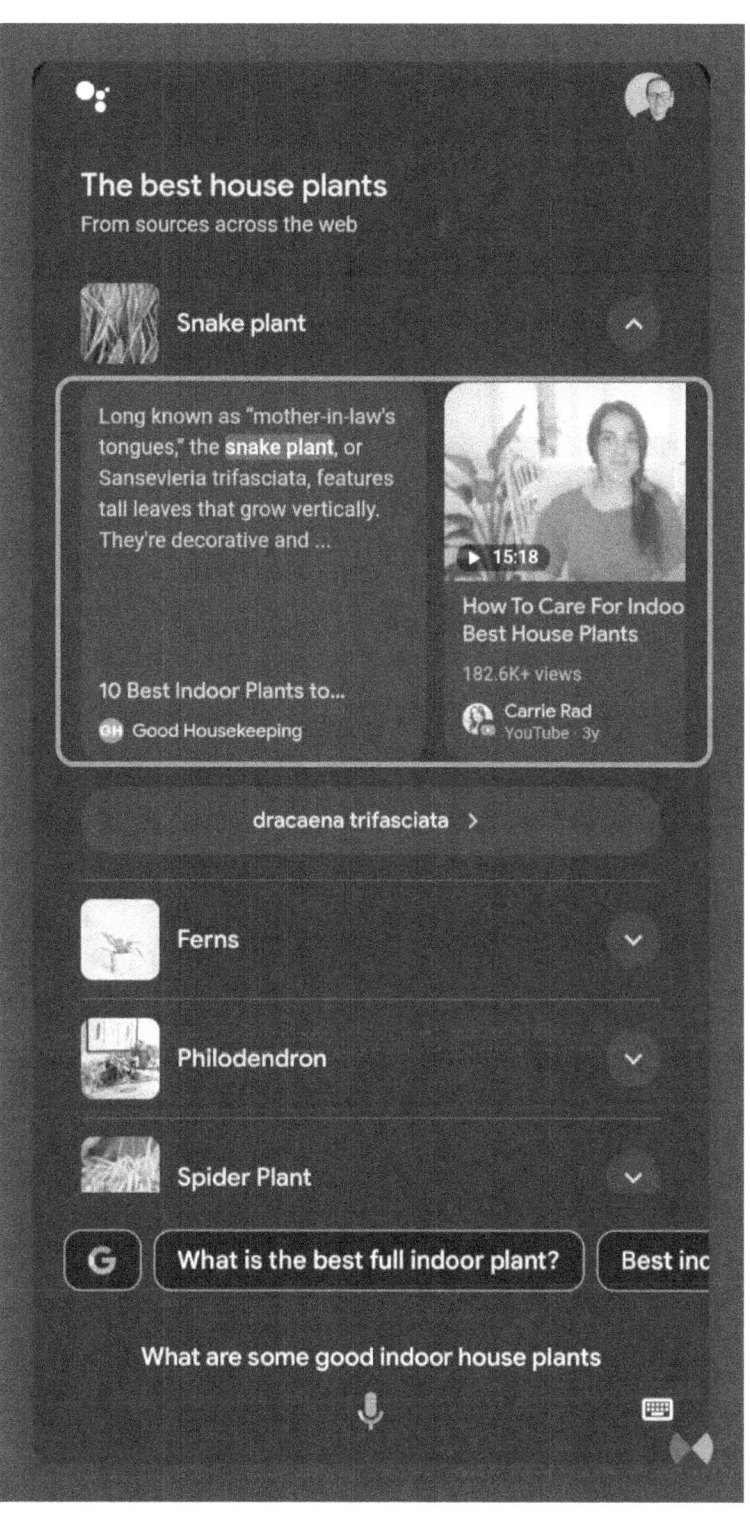

We will see more evolution of these features over time. Google is learning with each search whether people are finding AI Overviews helpful. They will continually learn how to improve.

Here's more reading:

- Google's documentation on SGE
- Google's June 2024 documentation on AI Overviews.
- Google's announcement about SGE
- You can also find all sorts of examples of SGE in action and community discussion on what it is rewarding in the Search Bar.

Google Gemini (formerly Bard)

Google's naming of products is confusing! You may have noticed that throughout this book I refer sometimes to Bard, and sometimes to Gemini. This is because in early 2024, Bard was renamed to Gemini. Gemini is *also* the name of the language model behind the system. Gemini essentially is everything that is AI at Google.

Gemini the chatbot is not a search engine. But people will likely use it as one. It is a way to get information, and the more it improves, the more helpful it becomes.

Gemini will become Google Assistant, and be available at a quick touch or voice command on most phones that can pop up over top of other apps.

It is continually improving via a process called reinforcement learning. If you used Bard a few times and gave up because you found it unhelpful, I'd encourage you to try out Gemini. Ideally it's worth signing up for the most advanced version of Gemini publicly available, Gemini Advanced[46]. As I write this, Google is offering a two month trial.

In the short time since Bard upgraded to Gemini I have been thoroughly impressed with its improvement. It feels like it improves daily.

In February of 2024 Google quietly announced an upgrade to Gemini called **Gemini 1.5** that gives it an entirely new architecture based on something called a Mixture of Experts model. This type of model is not new, but DeepMind says that the type of MoE model they use for Gemini is a brand new version of MoE. The changes made to Gemini made it *significantly* more efficient, accurate and better able to understand the data it trains on.

Gemini 1.5 greatly improves Google's AI capabilities across the board. And creates a framework for them to continue to improve at a fast rate.

Here are some helpful links to learn more about Gemini:

- Use Gemini.
- Google's announcement re Bard.

---

[46] Gemini Advanced. https://gemini.google.com/advanced

- How Google's multimodal Gemini model makes Bard much better.
- Could Bard One Day Replace the Google Search Box?
- On Bard extensions.
- Challenge: Can you get your site to surface in Bard's double-check response suggestions?
- Some thoughts on Retrieval Augmented Generation (RAG) and how Google's search results are structured to make Bard better.

If you read one thing on Gemini, make it this:

Google's Blog post called, "Assistant with Bard: A step toward a more personal assistant."

I thoroughly believe Gemini is the way of the future. It might not seem like it if you have used it a few times and run into a few hallucinations and made up answers. After reading all of the above, hopefully you will see what I see and that is that Gemini is poised to be the future of how we interact with information online.

A lot will likely change in the world as this happens.

How? It's hard to predict. I think that many people will be affected like I have been. The more I use LLM's, the more I learn. The more I learn, the more knowledge I have. Then I can take those ideas and brainstorm them with Gemini or ChatGPT. This has led to me being able to understand a lot about how Search works and to develop my skills in almost everything I do in my work at a faster pace. The more I do this, the more I learn how to learn and also to get the most out of the LLM tools that are available to me.

People who are good at their trades will get better with the help of AI. Those who know how to use AI will start to develop significant advantages over those who do not. Imagine if you were living in 2024 and did not use a phone. You could certainly live, but you would be at a disadvantage compared to those who do use technology.

I believe we may face a dangerous divide in our civilization as this happens. I am beyond excited for those who are at the cutting edge of learning how we can improve the world with AI. But what will happen to those who decide to avoid its use at all costs?

Fortunately, Google's CEO has said that this transition in how we search will happen [over the next decade](). We hopefully have some time to adjust.

Business integration

In Google's earnings calls they have mentioned that one of Gemini's strengths is business integration. We haven't seen it yet. But eventually, we should see it get easier and easier for businesses to not only integrate Google's AI capabilities, but also make money from it.

Pay attention to how AI is changing Google Ads as well. I have not written about Ads in this book, but can see all sorts of future opportunities here.

Let me share what I think could happen. Imagine a searcher is looking for information on a recent traffic drop. They converse with Gemini, who tells them the world's general advice about what to consider and then recommends perhaps some websites to read. I could see Google offering paid positions that say, **"Talk to Marie Haynes' AI Assistant"**. It's an Ad that then connects the searcher with a chatbot on my site. This chatbot would be grounded with my recent writings. I would be incentivized to continue to create great, helpful content because this is what will make my chatbot useful. It's possible I could charge money for this chatbot. Or, perhaps I might choose to make it free and where appropriate, the chatbot would recommend my resources and services. In that case, I could see Google inserting my Chatbot right into the search results.

When businesses start to make real money from Google's AI, we will see some more acceleration!

AGI / ASI

If you have heard of AGI, Artificial General Intelligence, or ASI, Artificial Super Intelligence, the idea likely conjures up images of fearful possibilities. We're used to hearing stories about terminators and evil people crafting plans to destroy the world with an AI system gone rogue. To finish this book, I would like to try to convince you that our future is likely to be *incredible* because of AGI.

There is not a general consensus on what the definition of AGI is amongst AI leaders. The 2023 Expert Survey on Progress in AI[47] surveyed 2,778 AI researchers from top-tier venues to gather their predictions on the pace of AI progress and the nature and impacts of advanced AI systems. In this paper, they define AGI in terms of "High-Level Machine Intelligence" (HLMI) where an occupation becomes fully automatable by unaided machines and more cheaply than human workers."

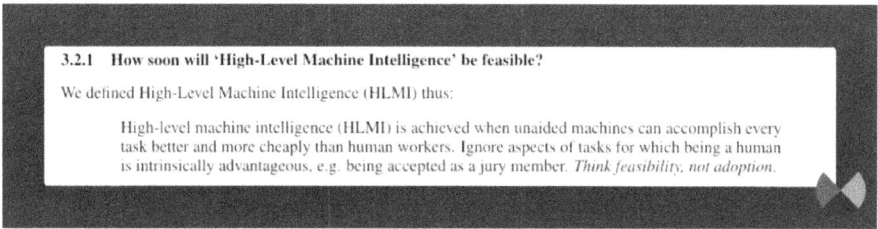

Between 2022 and 2023 the aggregate forecast of the AI researchers on when HLMI would arrive dropped by 13 years.

---

[47] Thousands of AI authors on the future of AI. https://aiimpacts.org/wp-content/uploads/2023/04/Thousands_of_AI_authors_on_the_future_of_AI.pdf

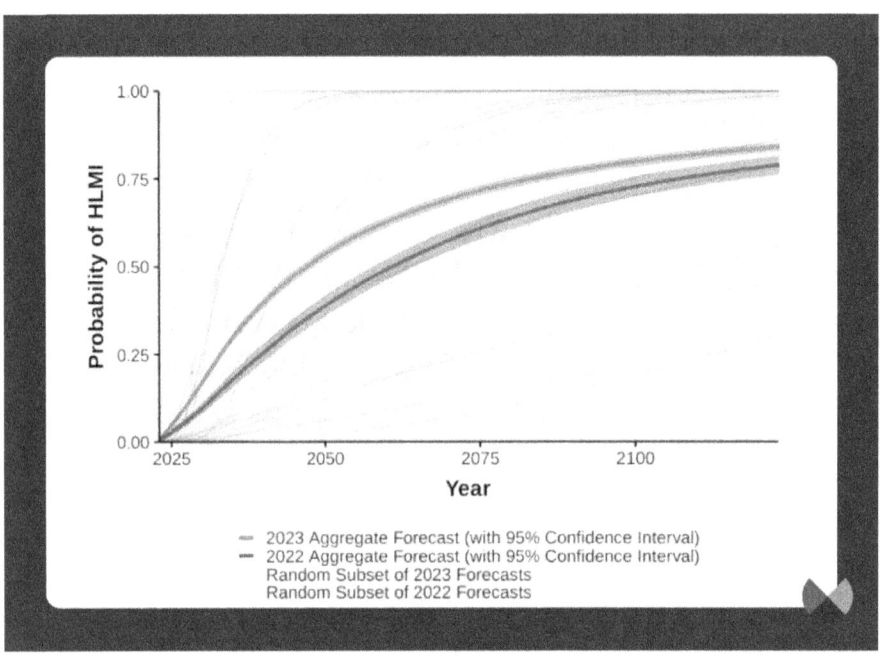

Demis Hassabis, the founder of DeepMind, which was one of the leading forces behind Google's development of Gemini, says that to him AGI is a system that is able to do "pretty much any cognitive task that humans can do[48]."

DeepMind's mission is to work towards building AGI as they say it has the **potential to drive one of the greatest transformations in history.**[49]

---

[48] Demis Hassabis on Chatbots to AGI | Ep 71. Hard Fork. https://www.youtube.com/watch?v=nwUARJeeplA

[49] Build AI responsibly to benefit humanity. Google Deep Mind's About page. https://deepmind.google/about/

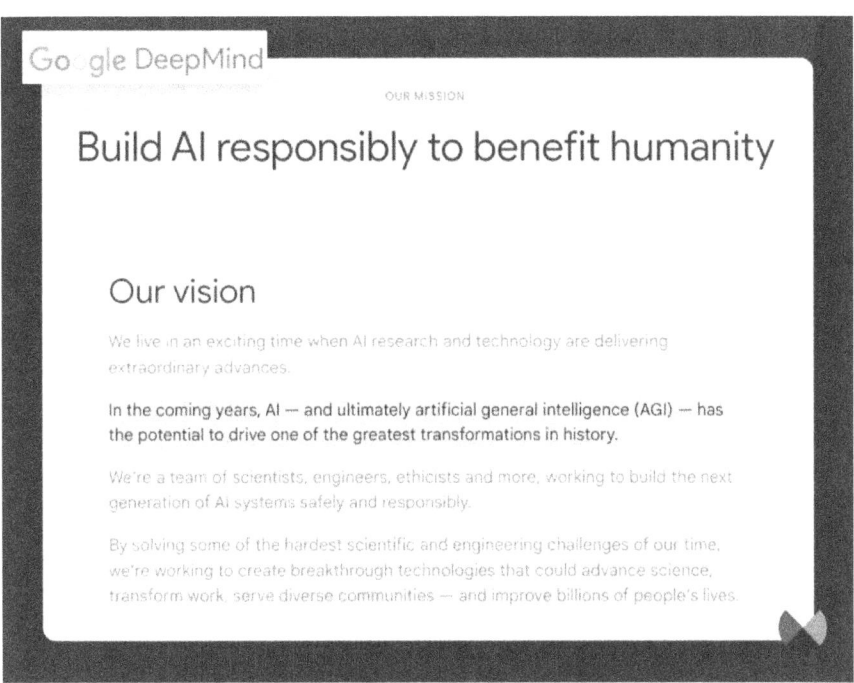

Sundar Pichai, Google's CEO has said multiple times that **AI technology is more profound than electricity or fire**[50].

Those are some big words!

When is Google expected to get to AGI?

Demis Hassabis says Google still has a way to go before they've created AGI, but they are "making enormous progress with Gemini and those types of systems which [he thinks] will be important components of an AGI system."

---

[50] Google CEO: AI more important to humanity than fire, electricity. NBC News. https://www.nbcnews.com/video/google-ceo-sundar-pichai-on-a-i-being-more-important-technology-than-electricity-1141192259992

"I would not be surprised if we saw systems nearing that kind of capability within the next decade or sooner."

Coincidentally, in Google's 2023 Q3 earnings call, Sundar Pichai spoke of Google's "opportunity to evolve Search with Assistant over **the next decade ahead**[51].

A decade is a long time..perhaps? But Hassabis hints that this change could come even sooner.

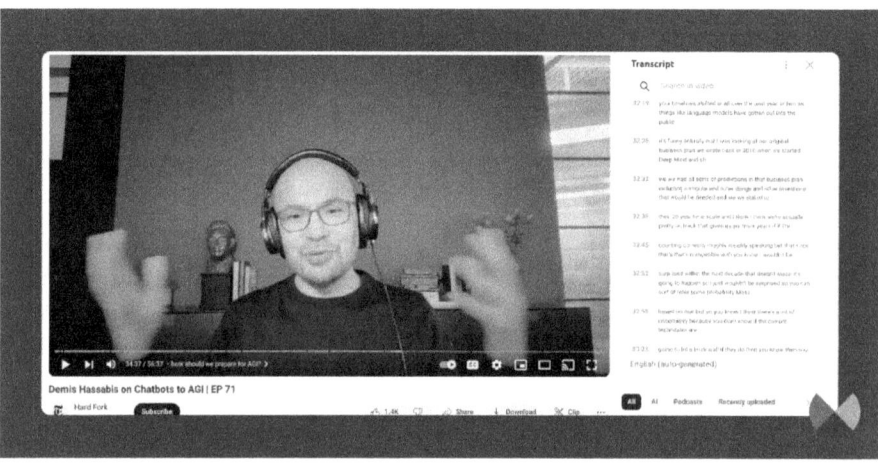

He said he was looking at his original business plan they wrote back in 2010 when starting Deep Mind in 2010. They predicted what would be needed to build AGI, and then predicted this would happen on a 20-year time scale. He said, "I think we're actually pretty on track. **That gives us six more years** if I'm counting correctly. Roughly, roughly speaking, but

---

[51] What we learned about SGE, Bard and Gemini from Google's Q3 2023 Earnings call. Marie Haynes. October 26, 2023.
https://www.mariehaynes.com/what-we-learned-about-sge-bard-and-gemini-from-googles-q3-2023-earnings-call/

that's compatible with, you know, I wouldn't be surprised within the next decade…"

I do believe Google is working towards building AGI, and that they have been, perhaps since the beginning of their quest to organize the world's information and make it universally accessible.

This is why it is so important for Google to get things right when it comes to recommending information that is helpful and reliable.

If you have been working as an SEO, you have been helping businesses improve how they present themselves as among those helpful and reliable resources. We initially learned how to create content that looked good to search engines. Then, over the last twenty five years Google has learned from this content and slowly, with incremental improvements, they've worked closer and closer towards the goal Larry Page told us about in 2000 when he said that artificial intelligence would be the future of Google[52].

[52] Larry Page talking about AI in 2000.
https://www.youtube.com/shorts/62SbHWql-1U

He said, "**Artificial Intelligence would be the ultimate version of Google. So if we had the ultimate search engine, it would understand everything on the web. It would understand exactly what you wanted and it would give you the right thing.**"

There are so many questions that can be asked about AGI. I think that discussing how it is likely to change our future is like asking the first people who learned about electricity's ability to light up the filament in a light bulb to predict electric self-driving cars, space travel, or smartphones and the internet.

Still, let's dream of how AGI is expected to change our lives. I gave the text I have written here to Gemini and asked it to complete this for me.

 Here are 5 brief bullet points describing how AGI could improve our lives:

- **Accelerated scientific breakthroughs:** AGI could analyze massive datasets, discover unseen patterns, and design complex experiments, leading to faster medical cures, clean energy solutions, and a deeper understanding of the universe.
- **Personalized and revolutionized education:** AGI-powered tutors could adapt to each student's learning style and pace, providing limitless opportunities for truly individualized education.
- **Enhanced problem-solving in complex fields:** AGI systems could optimize logistics, resource allocation, and city planning, leading to greater efficiency, sustainability, and improved quality of life.
- **Unleashed Creativity:** AGI could collaborate with humans as a creative partner, assisting in artistic endeavors like music composition, writing, and design, opening up new forms of expression.
- **Freeing humans from tedious tasks:** AGI could handle mundane or dangerous jobs, allowing humans to focus on more fulfilling work, leisure, and interpersonal connection.

There is so much more we need to discuss on AGI, or even on AI as it advances towards AGI.

Am I worried about the potential for AI to do harm in society? While I think this technology will overall help billions of people have much better lives, I do worry about the path that we will take to get there. I think we are entering a period where those who understand how AI works will have all sorts of advantages over those who choose to ignore it. At the same time many people will have their jobs displaced because of AI, or will find themselves disadvantaged because of the way the world is shifting how we interact with machines.

We are already seeing new ways to disseminate disinformation. In theory, there is a non-zero percentage chance that the development of AI turns into something that could destroy humanity.

If that is the case, why pursue AI development at all?

I do not think we have a choice.

Humanity has been surging forward for thousands of years now, all in an effort to continually improve upon technology.

In 3500 or so BC, sand was first formed into glass, and at nearly the same time humans in Mesopotamia and Egypt were creating the beginnings of this incredible system that today we call **math**.

We learned how to turn silicon to glass, which allowed us to improve eyesight, extending productive years for scholars. Eventually glass led to us creating microscopes and telescopes, which let us peer into unseen worlds and further understand the laws that govern our world. Our understanding of math and physics that came from studying the planets laid the foundation for classical mechanics and underpins the design of everything from simple machines to complex engineering projects like bridges, aircraft and rockets.

Einstein pushed innovation even further, taking the world's knowledge and understanding of Neutonian physics to create his theory of relativity in which the movement of objects can be predicted by understanding **their relationships within the fabric of space and time**.

Is this beginning to sound familiar? It should because this is essentially the same concept we have been discussing when we talked about how the relationships in data are captured in vector spaces. Vector spaces are using numbers to represent the relationships between things.

Humanity has been striving for thousands of years to turn sand into intelligence.

Today, we do it with silicon in chips, the very same element that gave us the glass to see the stars.

We can choose to ignore what is coming. We can take a stance to point out the faults or dangers of AI as it grows. But I can guarantee you the world will not be reaching out for help from those who criticize AI, but rather from those who have **some type of understanding of what is going on**.

I am well aware of the potential dangers of AI. I decided that I cannot stop AI from progressing, so I want to do all I can to learn how to help people use it to its full potential to do good in the world. And also I want to get people excited about doing good with AI!

Because my business revolved around helping websites that had suffered because of changes in Google' systems, it has led me to deeply study and be able to explain what is happening with Google's systems. I am seeing what is likely the beginning of significant job displacement as a result of the changes that AI brings.

I would encourage you to spend time reading this report from Google on the expected economic impact of AI:

https://storage.googleapis.com/gweb-uniblog-publish-prod/documents/Generally_Faster_-_The_Economic_Impact_of_Generative_AI.pdf

They say AI will reduce demand for some skill, increase demand for others and create demand for entirely new ones. They repeatedly refer to the urgent need for the "reskilling" of the workforce that will be needed. There is so much opportunity on the horizon!

If you ask Google what to focus on following a drop in traffic following a Google update, their replies may seem a little glib for an SEO who has diligently followed traditional SEO advice and practices. But now that we understand that Google's recommendations are driven by an AI system that is built to predict what people are likely to find helpful and reliable, these tweets make more sense.

"Make pages for users not search engines" - Google, 2002

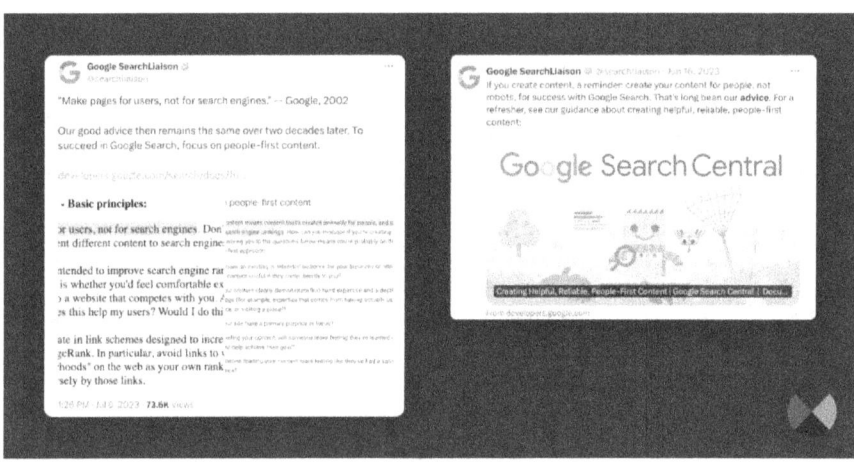

Google Search Liaison tweets from July 2023 - Make pages for users, not for search engines -- Google has been saying this since 2002.[53]

It seems clear to me that Search as we know it today is just a step in the road towards Google building a good AI assistant, and likely one day, AGI - a system smarter than us, but yet working with us to improve humanity.

---

[53] Google Search Liason on X.
https://x.com/searchliaison/status/1677006067098845185?s=20,
https://x.com/searchliaison/status/1669752862099009540?s=20

We will one day think of Search with nostalgia, just like when I think of my first few emergency phone calls I received on a cell phone in a gigantic black bag on the floor of my car in my early days as a veterinarian on call. Or, the feel of dialing a rotary phone.

One day we may even marvel at the time when we used our ***fingers*** to search. We have not yet begun to speak of how the world changes once we have AGI that is available at the tap of an earbud, or perhaps even by triggering it with a thought. Meta is making significant progress on a [wearable like a wristwatch](#) that takes just the thought of typing and turns it into communication with our computers. They predict we'll be able to type with our thoughts five times faster than we currently can with our fingers.

Imagine the number of times my muscles have made my fingers dance across this thing we use called a keyboard while I have written this book. Again, one day, a relic of the past, just like pen and paper, rotary telephones, the telegraph, writing letters, town criers, and traveling bards telling stories.

There is one thing that has been important, always has been, and for as far as I can see in the future, *will continue to be*, and that is **creating great content to share helpful knowledge**. Long time SEO's will remember the endless memes where Google's head of webspam, Matt Cutts' answer to every question years ago, was essentially a version of "create great content."

Now this makes more sense!

10 years ago Matt spoke about the initial blog post[54], written by Amit Singhal at Google that lists the "Panda Questions", similar to today's helpful content questions, saying, "It talks about the sorts of signals that we look at whenever we're trying to assess quality within Panda." Also, **"If you think you might be affected by Panda, the overriding kind of goal is to try to make sure that you've got high quality content. The sort of content that people enjoy, that's compelling. The sort of thing that they'll love to read, that you might see in a magazine or in a book, and that people would refer back to, or send friends to."**

If you are reading this book, you likely have played a role in creating AGI by creating or advising on creating content on the internet in ways that Google's systems are likely to reward. You've helped Google learn to organize the world's information.

You may be thinking that perhaps Google has swindled us all. They've trained us to create content, and then they've taken all of this content to create an AI system without any recompense to the site owners who made it.

I think the world is headed in this direction regardless, whether it was Google or some other AI company that leads the way.

---

[54] More guidance on building high-quality sites. Google Search Central Blog. Amit Singhal. May 6, 2011.
https://developers.google.com/search/blog/2011/05/more-guidance-on-building-high-quality

I thoroughly believe that Google will make changes to make it quite lucrative for those who truly do create the type of content that people are hungry to consume. Google's AI needs fresh content. They need to know what topic experts are saying.

I have many ideas on how Google will do this and could write a whole extra book on this. For now I'd encourage you to keep an eye on the following:

- NotebookLM[55]. This AI tool from Google allows you to upload documents, images, and urls and then query them. I can see this turning into a way for people to make money by sharing their knowledge and data.
- AI driven changes to ads[56]. Google says we are in a new era of AI-powered ads. I expect that interesting opportunities will open up here. I can picture a day where I can say, "Make an app that uses the knowledge from my website and these instructions based on my wisdom on a topic to solve this particular problem for my audience." And I expect that in an age where AI generated content is cheap, using AI to interact with the content of true topic experts sharing uniquely valuable knowledge on their topics will be something quite valuable. Imagine ads that allow you to

---

[55] NotebookLM: https://notebooklm.google/
[56] Introducing a new era of AI-powered ads with Google. Google Ads & Commerce Blog. https://blog.google/products/ads-commerce/ai-powered-ads-google-marketing-live/ May 23, 2023

essentially speak with an expert's assistant, trained on their content and ongoing knowledge on a topic.
- **Hyper Personalized results**. I believe we will see more changes in our search results to reflect the types of sites we want to read from. There is a lot to get right here, so this may not come right away. But if it does, it will open up all sorts of opportunities for content creators who have an audience that is hungry for their content.
- **Video**. I don't think we've yet seen the full power of Gemini to understand which video content on pages truly is helpful to people. It's coming. I think there will be all sorts of opportunities for those who can create truly helpful video that AI can't replicate. Pay close attention to YouTube's connection to Shopify. There are all sorts of things happening here. And pay close attention to YouTube shorts and television.
- **Micropayments.** In February of 2024, the Register reported that the team behind Google Chrome is working on a micropayments system that will allow content creators to be paid for their content[57]. This could turn into something quite interesting.
- **Google Reader Revenue Manager**[58]. I got really excited when I first heard of this program. Since its announcement on this program, Google has done very

---

[57] Chrome engine devs experiment with automatic browser micropayments. Thomas Claburn. The Register. Feb 13, 2024.
https://www.theregister.com/2024/02/13/google_micropayments_plan/

[58] Grow your revenue and deepen your reader engagement. Google Reader Revenue Manager. https://readerrevenue.withgoogle.com/

little to push this to site owners. I believe this is for good reason. Once we have more capabilities to easily use AI to let our audience interact with our content, *then* we should have all sorts of incentives to create helpful content. For example, I could see a system where I would be encouraged to write all helpful content on the helpful content system, and then, I could give access to an AI tool built with Gemini and trained on my content alongside. This is something worth paying for. Because it uses Google Cloud, it would cost me money and make Google money. Because it is likely to be helpful, this type of a service is something that could lead to book sales, further consulting or other business. I predict all sorts of ways for creative people to make money from their content.

- Google AI studio[59]. This is geared towards developers. For now, it's not super easy to use, but boy is it worthwhile to spend time trying to figure out how. This is the beginning of the way that we will take natural language and use Google's AI to turn it into apps. I'd encourage you to play around with creating structured prompts to help you accomplish tasks that you use AI for regularly.
- Vertex AI[60]. Again, this is for developers, but if you have even the slightest interest in building with AI you should be poking around in here. In Google's earnings calls they have bragged how one of Gemini's strengths

---

[59] Google AI studio. https://aistudio.google.com/app/prompts/new_chat
[60] Vertex AI. https://cloud.google.com/vertex-ai

is integration for businesses. We have not seen this yet, but I expect that those who understand how to build things in Vertex AI will be quite sought after! I would especially pay attention to the new Generative AI powered search and conversational experiences with [Gen App Builder](#)[61]. I expect we will soon see businesses doing all sorts of wild and creative things with Google's AI technology as it becomes more readily available and easy to integrate.

A new age for content...and everything really!

I thoroughly believe we are entering into a new age when it comes to creating content to be found online - the Gemini Age.

Google's AI driven systems are now powered by AI technology that continues to learn and improve when it comes to recognizing which content is likely to satisfy a searcher's needs.

---

[61] Build new generative AI powered search & conversational experiences with Gen App Builder. March 29, 2023. https://cloud.google.com/blog/products/ai-machine-learning/create-generative-apps-in-minutes-with-gen-app-builder

I mean, they *have been* powered by AI for years now. But Gemini 1.5 changes the game making these systems even more powerful.

And here's the thing.

In order for AI to continue to be useful, it needs data that it does not yet already have.

Many who are reading this book have been diligently creating content that **essentially already exists**, when Google says they want to reward content that is original, insightful and truly helpful. This is why some of Google's helpful content questions say,

- If the content draws on other sources, does it avoid simply copying or rewriting those sources, and instead provide **substantial additional value and originality**?
- Is this the sort of page you'd want to bookmark, share with a friend, or recommend?
- Does the content provide substantial value when compared to other pages in search results?

One of the problems is that this transition to become the AI engine that Google aims to be has been slow and is not yet complete. You may look at some of your search results and think that they are unhelpful and that Google has gotten worse rather than better. Or, you may argue that what remains in the search results after your site was demoted is no more original than your content is. And perhaps you are correct! Or, perhaps the results truly *are* getting closer to what people want to find and not what search engines used to reward.

I expect though that if you look at your search results as a whole, you will find that Google is ranking content that comes from sites that are either authoritative, have topic expertise, or truly are helpful content that a searcher would want to see even once they've been given an answer by their AI assistant. This is the type of content that we have been talking about producing, throughout this book.

I hope that this book helps you make web pages that are so helpful that Google would be embarrassed not to show them to people. But really I hope for more than that.

Your purpose is so much more than just ranking websites.

I want to finish this book with more on my conversation with Jeff Dean. We talked about the brain and newly published research from Google and Harvard that showed incredible imagery of the brain[62] with the help of AI.

The team of neuroscientists who did this work reconstructed nearly every cell of a section of brain tissue about half the size of a grain of rice. Along with the cells, they were able to visualize every connection between them. Some neurons were found to have over 50 of these connections, called synapses. Look at how beautiful this neuron is. There are more than 5000 axons (blue) bringing signals from other neurons.

---

[62] 6 incredible images of the human brain built with the help of Google's AI. https://blog.google/technology/research/google-ai-research-new-images-human-brain/

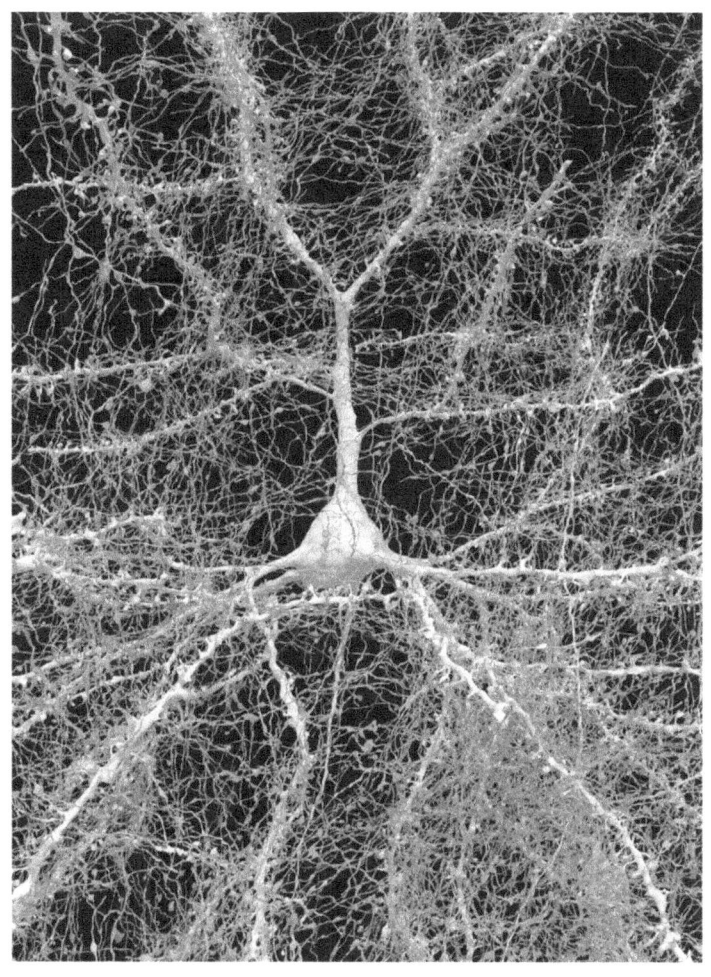

This is the part that I could not stop looking at:

6. Serious networking

A single neuron (white) receives signals that determine whether or not the neuron fires. This image shows all of the axons that can tell it to fire (green) and all of those that can tell it not to (blue). Multiply this by the whole brain and that's a lot of talking!

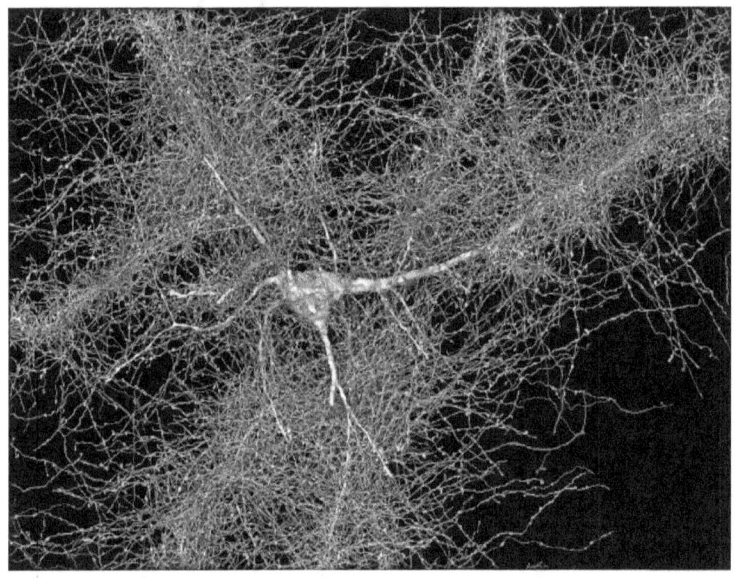

Credit: Google Research & Lichtman Lab (Harvard University). Renderings by D. Berger (Harvard University)

What struck me, and was that the brain is essentially a Mixture of Experts model! It is a network of neural networks, all working together and firing as needed.

Jeff said, "Yes, a *sparse* Mixture of Experts." He should know as, he authored the paper referenced in Google's Gemini 1.5 announcement[63], Outrageously Large Neural Networks: the Sparsely-Gated Mixture-of-Experts layer.[64]

---

[63] Our next-generation model: Gemini 1.5. The Keyword.

I asked Gemini, which by the way was named by Jeff[65], to help me explain how Google's new AI architecture is so similar to that of the brain.

> Show drafts ⌄
>
> A sparse MoE model, like the one powering Google's Gemini 1.5, is a multifaceted AI powerhouse that deftly juggles multiple specialized neural networks, each excelling at distinct tasks. This intricate dance of expertise is orchestrated by a sophisticated gating network, which intelligently determines the optimal combination of experts to tackle any given query. By activating only the most relevant experts for each unique search, Gemini 1.5 unlocks unprecedented levels of efficiency and precision, transforming the search experience by delivering tailored results that are both comprehensive and lightning-fast.

We have entered a new era of Search. One in which the math of multiple machine learning systems is orchestrated like a symphony by Google's brain for ranking, RankBrain.

This brain is learning to organize the world's information and make it universally accessible. This process started 25 years ago with Larry Page's dream to download and make ranking calculations from the links on the web.

---

https://blog.google/technology/ai/google-gemini-next-generation-model-february-2024/#gemini-15

[64] Outrageously Large Neural Networks: The Sparsely-Gated Mixture-of-Experts Layer. Noam Shazeer, Azalia Mirhoseini, Krzysztof Maziarz, Andy Davis, Quoc Le, Geoffrey Hinton, Jeff Dean. Jan 2017. https://arxiv.org/abs/1701.06538

[65] How Google's AI model Gemini got its name. The Keyword. https://blog.google/technology/ai/google-gemini-ai-name-meaning/

205

As SEOs we have played a role in teaching the businesses and creators of this world how to be found online. This role does not change!

What does change is the landscape. We don't know what the future holds. We do know that businesses will continue to exist and new opportunities will open up as the world learns what we can do with the help of AI.

We will one day think of Search with nostalgia, similar to remembering visits to the Library. The world will continue to need access to more and more information. As AI develops it will get much more important to understand which entities in the world truly do have Experience, Expertise, Authoritativeness and Trustworthiness. Those who understand E-E-A-T will have a better understanding of what's true and worthy of our attention.

I am so excited to continue to learn about how our world is changing. It has been an honour to be able to share my thoughts with you. I wish you the best of luck with your rankings and really with EVERYTHING.

We are in for an exciting time!

Marie

www.ingramcontent.com/pod-product-compliance
Lightning Source LLC
Chambersburg PA
CBHW082233220526
45479CB00005B/1215